A
Basic Foil
Companion

FENCING MASTER PAUL SISE

A
Basic Foil
Companion

by Paul Sise
Prévôt d'Armes, Maître Escrime Epee
US Fencing Coaches Association and International Academy of Arms
(Provost at Arms, Master of Epee Fencing)

Photographs by Jennifer Holmes

SKA SwordPlay Books
Staten Island, NY

A Basic Foil Companion

© 2010 Paul Sise

ISBN 978-0-9789022-5-4

Photographs by Jennifer Holmes

Illustrations on pp. 45 – 46 courtesy of and copyright Blade Fencing Equipment, Inc.

Scoresheet on pp. 52-53 and classification chart on page 55 © US Fencing Association

Illustrations on p. 36 © Fédération Internationale d'Escrime

SKA SwordPlay Books

3939 Victory Boulevard

Staten Island, NY 10314

Visit our website at www.swordplaybooks.com

Contents

Dedication

I dedicate this book to my students, past and present, who have over the years both suffered through and enjoyed my classes. This book is, first and foremost, for all of you.

Special Thanks

I'd like to give special thanks to the people who have both directly and indirectly made this book possible: to Annie McRae for modeling the parry positions and other fencing actions, to Jennifer Holmes for taking many of the photographs, to Wendell Kubik for his Preface to the book (I hope that he enjoys the final product as much as he did the early draft that he read.) Thanks to Ken Mondschein for helping proofread the text. Thanks – last, but not least – to my wife, Karen, for her support.

I'd also like to thank my instructors who have educated and trained me as a fencer and a coach, including various members of the US Fencing Coaches Association (USFCA) and instructors at the USFA Coaches College, in particular Gary Copeland. Whether he realizes it or not, Gary has made a significant impact on my development as a coach.

Finally, it is only fitting to thank Steve and Barbara Khinoy, who have not only done the hard job of turning my simple text into a book, but who have also offered me their encouragement and excitement over it.

Preface

By Wendell Kubik, Past President, US Fencing Coaches Association

Let's face it: most foil manuals are boring! It's a good thing fencing is fun because if I had judged my early fencing experience on the foil books I had read, I might not have made it as a fencer or a coach.

This handbook by Paul Sise introduces foil skills in plain language that is easy for youth fencers or adult beginners to understand. This manual is full of helpful hints and all the usual stuff that is covered during the first year of instruction by experienced coaches.

It doesn't favor a particular school of thought or method of instruction, so it should complement most beginning foil classes. It will also stimulate some good discussion in class and always encourages the reader to consult the coach for specifics.

I like the chapter on choosing a handle or grip for your foil. Many coaches favor one handle over others. I have learned over the years that beginners learn just as effectively with pistol grips as with the traditional foil grips. The emphasis on finger control is explained very well.

The photos are clear and serve as helpful reminders for beginners.

This is a guide that a beginning fencer can keep in their equipment bag and go back to over the years. It answers a lot of the questions that come up during the first year of fencing with clear and easy to remember explanations. I wish I had a handbook like this to offer to my fencers during the many foil classes I taught over the years.

Wendell Kubik, Fencing Master
Past President, US Fencing Coaches Association
Past Chairman, US Fencing Youth Development Committee
Past Chairman, NCAA Men's Fencing Committee

Introduction

Welcome to fencing! By learning the fine art, science, and sport of fencing you are joining a tradition that spans the centuries. Fencing is a challenging activity that can keep testing you and rewarding you throughout your whole life.

Years ago, I was at an activities fair where I had a booth set up to advertise my fencing club. An old man with a cane saw my booth as he hobbled slowly by. He made his way over to me and I stood up to greet him. My first thought was that he was going to ask about signing up his grandkids (or possibly his great-grandkids) for classes. (A few people had already signed up that morning.) I was wrong. He smiled and shook my hand and asked if he could hold a foil. I handed him one and he swung it around a bit and fondly told me about how he had taken a fencing class as a Boy Scout about seventy-five years ago. It was the only time he had done it, but he carried happy memories from it his whole life. It was unlike anything else he had ever done. He hadn't held a foil since that summer as a Boy Scout, but he told me that he still thought of himself as a fencer. It was something we shared. We had something in common.

As a fencer, you can be at home anywhere in the world!

Fencing is a very old sport with a rich and colorful history that's covered elsewhere far better than I could ever attempt. It is an Olympic sport and is practiced around the world. Today there is a vibrant and growing community of fencers that want the sport they love to continue to grow and strengthen. As a fencer you are now part of that community; and believe it or not, you are important to it. Fencers around the world who have never met you are proud of you for learning to fence and would, if they could, shake your hand, pat your back, and thank you for joining them. Wherever you go, you can be sure that there is a place for you to be welcomed and appreciated. You might even be visiting a foreign country and not know the language, but at the fencing club, with a foil in your hand, you can feel that you are at home.

In your class there is going to be a lot to learn, so pay close attention, and at the end of each session, take some notes on what you did. You may also wish to write down a few questions for the next session. The various topics covered may include fencing equipment, safety, rules, how to move back and forth on the strip with footwork, how to do various offensive, counteroffensive, and defensive techniques with the blade, strategy or tactics, sport psychology, and history.

It will be up to your coach to demonstrate how the actions are performed. He will also correct your mistakes, which is something no book can do. This companion guide is meant to be just that, a *companion* to the work you will be doing in your classes, not a substitute for your coach. This book will reinforce what the instructor is teaching you, give you something to study between classes (particularly vocabulary), and help you gauge your progress. There are usually several correct ways to do something. If this book disagrees with what your coach is teaching you, follow your coach's advice.

During the first few weeks, you may find yourself very excited about fencing and will be tempted to practice at home. Don't. I advise you to avoid practicing at home until your coach gives you permission to do so, because you will probably do yourself more harm than good without your coach or an experienced fencer to watch you and help correct you. Despite your good intentions, you'll be practicing mistakes. Over time, this can make mistakes habitual. That will frustrate not only you, but also your coach. If you'd like to do something at home to help your fencing you should jump rope, juggle, go dancing, or anything else that promotes fitness and agility.

Don't practice at home until your coach says you're ready. You could be practicing mistakes.

Finally, please do not wear jewelry such as large hoop earrings to the fencing club. Large rings, necklaces, and large earrings may cause discomfort, prevent the protective equipment from fitting properly, and may even create a safety hazard. Simple wedding bands, small stud earrings, and the like are usually OK. Do not wear makeup (or be sure to remove it before putting on your fencing gear). Makeup will rub off on the inside of the fencing mask and will be difficult to clean.

1. Sport Fencing and Stage Fencing

Swords have a long and colorful history. They have been wielded by conquerors, knights, and outlaws, by aristocrats, adventurers, and pirates, by generations of actors and actresses – and by athletes, the fencers of our own day. Most of us got our first glimpse of swordplay on the stage or screen. (Some of us immediately ventured into the back yard and dueled with broomsticks and garbage can lids.) Robin Hood and Zorro use swords; Darth Vader and Luke Skywalker wield Lightsabers. When swords are not available, the actors often reach for canes, umbrellas, or even loaves of French bread to fence each other.

Often enough, this fictional fencing inspires people to call up a local fencing club and sign up for a class. Visions of Zorro fade quickly as we find out that our lessons do not involve swinging from chandeliers, slicing through candles, or even wearing a cape. The romantic visions of the past give way to the Olympic sport of the present.

It turns out that learning to fence is hard work. It takes patience, determination, and sweat. It involves tiring repetition of actions. Some fencing classes don't even let students touch a weapon until they have completed several months of footwork lessons. In time though, with a good foundation of fundamentals, real-world fencers build up a repertoire of actions and strategies until they can do more than Zorro ever seems to.

The swordplay we usually see in movies or on the stage uses many of the same cutting, thrusting, and blocking actions that we use in sport fencing, but the concept behind the actions is very different. Swordfight scenes are meant to wow the audience. The actors leap and duck, clanging their blades in rapid and complicated patterns which are meticulously choreographed and rehearsed. They are also meant to be completely safe for the actors.

In other words, the fencing on stage and screen is almost the opposite of sport fencing. On stage, especially, an attacker wants to make it completely clear that a huge, sweeping cut is coming – clear to the audience, so that they can believe that the actor is in peril, and clear to the other actor, so that he can jump over it or duck under it and launch his own cut. If it's planned, rehearsed, and executed with ingenuity and skill, it's an exciting moment that looks completely spontaneous.

If you watch stage fencing carefully you may notice that the opponents are often too far apart to actually hit each other. Another difference from real fencing is that while fencers react to attacks with parries, actors tend to react to parries with attacks. One actor will move his blade to protect his left side, and just after he starts that action, the other actor begins his attack to that area, and from that we get a noisy and flashy – yet safe – swordplay phrase.

Fencers do, of course, care about safety, but unlike actors, we have clear safety rules; wear protective equipment and use weapons that are designed to do as little harm as possible. The good news is that, unlike actors, we are actually trying to hit each other. We don't clang our blades for the sake of show, and our actions are spontaneous instead of rehearsed. (It's also worth noting that our actions are really much faster!)

2. Foil, Saber, Epee

THE THREE WEAPONS

FOIL – A fencing weapon with a four-sided blade that uses the point to score touches. The target area is the torso of the opponent. Foil fencing uses rules of right of way.

EPEE – A fencing weapon with a three-sided blade that uses the point to score touches. The target area is the entire body of the opponent. Epee fencing does not use rules of right of way.

SABER – A fencing weapon that uses the point, edge, and sides of the blade to score touches. The target area is the torso, mask, and arms. Saber fencing uses rules of right of way similar to those of foil. Crossing the feet forward is illegal.

WHY FOIL?

Fencers compete in three weapons: foil, saber, and epee, yet most introductory fencing classes are foil classes. Much of this book is applicable to all three weapons, but it centers on beginning and intermediate foil.

Why foil? A word of explanation is in order.

For a long time, it was generally held that foil was the foundation weapon for fencing as a whole, and many fencing masters still hold to this principle. A year or two of foil training includes all the fundamentals of blade actions, footwork, and tactics. As a right of way weapon, with an emphasis on discipline, foil is thought to produce smarter, more wary fencers, no matter which weapon they eventually choose. In addition, foil is the link between epee (a thrusting weapon without right of way) and saber (a cutting and thrusting weapon with right of way). The foil is physically and mechanically like an epee. They are both point weapons (thrusting weapons) and use most of the same actions. But foil is also like saber in that both are right of way weapons. A student of foil therefore has the ability to move to epee (because it is a point weapon) or saber (because it is a *right-of-way* weapon) with less culture shock than say, a student of saber would have moving directly to epee (a thrusting-only weapon with no right of way.)

The link between epee and saber is that the target includes more than the torso: in epee, it's the entire body, from the head to the foot, while in saber, it includes everything above the waist except the hands. But the two weapons are fenced so differently that this link seems weaker than the links between foil and epee or foil and saber.

Another important consideration is that the foil is a light and flexible weapon that inflicts the least pain when it hits. The epee is stiffer, and uncontrolled saber slashes can really sting. Thus it is arguably the most appropriate weapon for newer fencers, particularly children. Finally, practice foils are fairly inexpensive and durable, and so foil is a cost-effective way of starting a recreational introductory class.

All of this can be debated, and it is being vigorously debated as I write this. Very young children usually don't have the fine motor control to perform the actions of a point weapon and would possibly do better in saber. In addition, competitive fencing has become more specialized. Success in more than one weapon at the international level is practically impossible, and even at the national and local levels, it is becoming rarer. There is competition in three weapons for younger and younger athletes, so that some programs encourage fencers to choose a weapon early.

CHOOSING YOUR WEAPON

So which weapon should you choose? This is one of the most interesting topics in fencing.

Certain stereotypes predict who fences which weapon.

Foil fencers are pictured as lean, quick, and interested in the creative artistry that takes place within a system of rules.

Epee fencers are pictured as tall, stubborn, crafty folk, who appreciate the freedom to act as they see fit rather than be "hindered" by the rules of right of way.

Saber fencers are pictured as being highly aggressive, a bit impulsive, and very quick, tending toward a solid athletic build with fast, powerful legs.

*Don't worry if you don't fit the stereotype for the weapon you like best. But **do ask** your coach.*

If you don't fit into any of these categories, don't worry. Plenty of champions didn't, either. All of these stereotypes have numerous exceptions. An experienced coach can usually offer advice to students about which weapon would fit them best based on their physical ability and personality. But in the end, the best advice is to choose the weapon that you love the most.

3. A Sample Syllabus

Some classes are six weeks long while others may go on for many months. What is taught in one beginner level class may be intermediate or advanced material in another. Whether or not your class follows this exact syllabus, you'll probably be taught this material at some point in your classes. The material will follow a logical order: learning attacks leads to learning parries; learning parries leads to learning feint attacks, etc.

Day 1: Footwork
On guard, advance, retreat, lunge, advance lunge
Paired footwork and distance drills
Demonstration of the different *distances*

Day 2: Simple Attacks
Getting gear and suiting up
The three *simple attacks (simple direct attack, disengage,* and *coupé.)*

Day 3: The Lines, Parries, and Ripostes
Discussion of the concept of *lines*
Parries 4 and 6 *lateral*
Riposte without *engagement*
Counter-ripostes

Fencing Vocabulary

All of the terms used in this sample syllabus will be discussed and defined. As you read, note the following:

When a term is being defined, or during the main discussion of the term, it looks like this:

PISTE – the fencing *strip.*

Italicizing *strip* indicates that **STRIP** appears as an entry in the Glossary.

Day 4: ROW and Continuations

Right of way (ROW) – what it is and how to get, give, and take ROW

Continuations of the attack: remise, reprise, and *redoublement*

Day 5: Attacks on the Blade

Press attack

Press (coach returns press) and disengage

Beat attack

Discussion of beats – their advantages and disadvantages

Day 6: More Parries and Indirect Riposte

Circular parries

Low line parries - parries 7 and 8

Parry-ripostes from 4, 6, 7 and 8

Indirect ripostes

Day 7: Point in Line and the Bind

Prise de fer against bent-armed opponent

Point in line

Transports – the *bind* or *diagonal transport*

Beat and bind against opponent using *point in line*

Riposte with *bind*

Day 8: Referee and Rules

The *referee*

Scoring and rules

Bouting

Day 9: Second Intention

Offensive second intention

Defensive second intention

Day 10: Feint Attacks

Feint attacks

Beat-feint-deceive of *parries* 4 and 6 both *lateral* and *circular*

4. Safety

Safety is everyone's responsibility. Fencing, like all sports, involves some risks. The club owner and coaches may be legally responsible for ensuring a safe environment, but it is up to everyone in the class to act safely and responsibly.

Use common sense. Never point a sword at someone who isn't wearing a mask. Accidents can happen of course, but we all do our best to prevent them. That means:

(1) **Inspect the environment** before using it. Are there wet and slippery spots on the floor? Is there enough space to fence without whacking the spectators?

(2) **Inspect the safety equipment.** Is the gear in good working order? Look for dents in the mask, holes in the uniform, kinks in the blades, etc. If something looks worn or broken, tell a coach; don't just put it back where you found it. Sometimes equipment can be easily repaired. Sometimes it can't.

(3) *Wear* **the safety equipment.** Just because you may have seen someone on TV fence without a mask on, that doesn't mean you should! Always wear your mask when blades are being used.

Can you spot all the safety hazards in the picture on the facing page?

(4) **Follow the rules of the club.** Each club will have its own rules, many of which deal with safety, such as where to store equipment, where to stand while watching, what to do with faulty equipment, etc.

(5) **Follow the rules of the sport and listen to your coach.** If the coach says to extend smoothly with the arm and hit the person gently on the chest you shouldn't wind up by cocking your elbow and slash with all your might.

(6) **Watch yourself – and your partner too.** You have the responsibility of fencing only when your partner is ready. He may be standing on guard in front of you, but if you see his collar undone, or his skin exposed, you should tell him. "Hey, you aren't supposed to be wearing shorts. Go put some pants on!"

(7) If you're not fencing, watch out for the fencers. They're focused on each other and aren't watching out for you.

Injuries in fencing are rare, but as in any sport, they do occur from time to time. If you are injured during fencing, inform the coach immediately.

Look at Fig. 1: "Unsafe!" and try to find the things that are unsafe about this fencer.

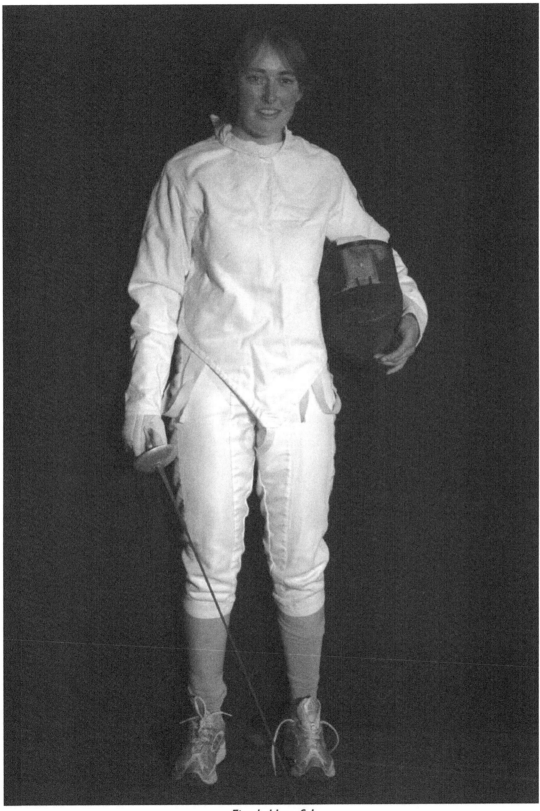

Fig. 1. Unsafe!

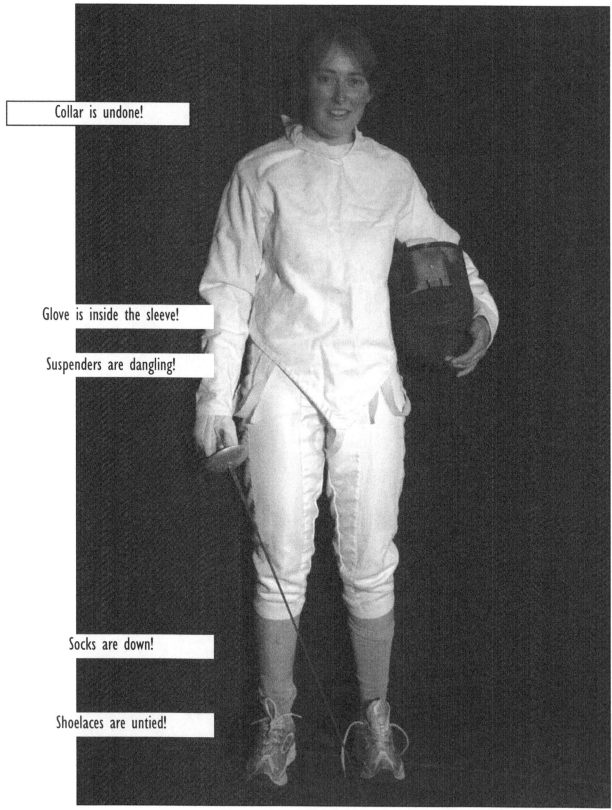

Fig. 1a. Unsafe! The safety hazards exposed.

5. Equipment

EQUIPMENT FOR PRACTICE AND INFORMAL BOUTING

If the club provides equipment, you most likely will need to arrive with just a T-shirt, sweat pants (since many clubs don't provide fencing *knickers* for beginner classes), and sneakers. You will probably also want to bring a water bottle and notebook. Men will need to provide their own *athletic cup*. Women provide themselves with some sort of breast protection. If you are a female student and need to buy your own equipment, or if your class does not provide one, I strongly suggest purchasing a *chestplate* as soon as possible. You may also wish to acquire a copy of the United States Fencing Association *(USFA)* Rulebook. You can do this by downloading it from their website, http://usfencing.org. At this website, you can find out much more about the sport, as well join the USFA on line.

Some clubs provide weapons as well as uniforms (sometimes called "the whites") as part of their beginner classes; some don't. In any case, if you stay with the sport, sooner or later you'll need to buy your own equipment. Uniforms and weapons are available in several grades of quality. Let's talk about the uniforms first.

Traditionally, fencing equipment required no certification. Non-certified equipment is generally considered trustworthy, and is legal for recreational, club, and competitive use within the U.S. It is frequently supplied in beginners' sets and offered by many college, school, and club fencing programs.

CE and FIE-approved items offer progressively better safety standards at a progressively higher weight – and price.

Next up the ladder is the increasingly popular *CE* (European) standard, tested and certified by an international European committee.

The highest grade of protection is the one required for international competition by fencing's world governing body, the *FIE*.

If you have to buy your own equipment, which do you choose? This may be a matter of budget for many fencers. If you don't know if you're going to continue fencing, or if you are a fast-growing kid, or if you are a purely recreational fencer or one who intends to compete only locally, you'd be fine selecting

> Parents of growing kids need to consider economics.
> But if you know you're going to stick with fencing, or go into competition, buy the best protection you can afford.

CE-certified or high-end non-certified gear. Personally, I always suggest that people buy the best protective equipment (uniform and mask) they can afford. If you can afford an FIE uniform it will be money well spent.

As for blades: FIE-approved blades have to be much more resistant to breaking than ordinary blades. Originally, all FIE blades were made of a specially-processed steel called maraging, so many people call them *maraging* blades. (However, not all Maraging blades meet FIE standards, and some non-Maraging blades pass the FIE tests.) FIE blades can cost at least twice as much as non-FIE blades, but they can last five times longer. If you can afford them, they are a good value. But once again: if you're just taking your first fencing class, you may not be ready to spring for FIE-approved weaponry, and that's OK.

Back to your first beginner class. Aside from T-shirt, sweat pants and sneakers, here's the gear you'll be using:

FENCING PANTS (OR KNICKERS) – Named from the word knickerbockers, meaning knee pants, these are worn by fencers in practice and competition. They go down to just below the knee, so you must wear long socks to cover the skin of the lower leg. The knickers must come up fairly high over the belly so that your skin is not exposed when your jacket rides up (for example, when you raise your arm over your head). Most knickers have suspenders. Many fencing clubs do not provide knickers and either require you to buy them or allow you to wear sweat pants. Sweat pants provide some protection but are not officially part of the fencing uniform, so it is best to be wearing knickers. (Note – In the UK, the word "knickers" refers to ladies undergarments. They call the fencing pants "breeches.")

ATHLETIC CUP FOR MEN – Provide your own. It is required by USFA rules for competition, and many clubs require it for practice.

LONG SOCKS – Socks must go up to meet the knickers and they must stay up. Some fencing companies sell fencing socks, but you can do as well with soccer socks or similar. They do not need to be white, and many fencers wear colorful socks to express themselves. Clubs and teams may have socks of specific color to help tell them apart from others.

SNEAKERS OR FENCING SHOES – Fencing shoes tend to be fairly light with thin but tough soles, a strong heel that squares off at the back to provide a stable landing for the front foot, and roll-over protection to prevent excessive wear on the rear shoe. Prices range from about $50 to over $200. You don't have to wear fencing shoes when you are starting out. Any good sneakers should suffice, particularly ones of the indoor soccer type. Try to avoid sneakers that make you feel like you are walking on thick pillows.

One important thing to remember is that whatever shoes you use for fencing, make sure they are dedicated solely to use in the fencing room. Don't wear them outside where they can pick up dirt and debris. The longer you stay in fencing, the more likely you are to choose specialized shoes.

CHESTPLATE (CHEST PROTECTOR) OR BREAST PROTECTORS FOR WOMEN - Required for women's fencing, the chestplate (chest protector) is a molded piece of plastic that covers the chest. It comes in various sizes. It is worn over the T-shirt, either under or over the underarm protector, and (by rule in competition) under the *fencing jacket.* **BREAST PROTECTORS** are small bowls. They are usually inserted into the pockets on the inside of a women's fencing jacket, but some women prefer to insert them into their sports bra for better fit.

Chestplates offer better fit and protection than breast protectors, but are hotter and more expensive. They are increasingly preferred.

CHESTPLATE (CHEST PROTECTOR) FOR BOYS AND MEN – The chestplate or chest protector is not required for men by the rules of fencing. It is worn over the T-shirt, either under or over the underarm protector, and (by rule in competition) under the *fencing jacket.* Strong hits to the sternum do not hurt while using a chestplate. They are very helpful for young boys who tend to flinch when being attacked. They offer a side benefit: the opponent's foil sometimes bounces off the chestplate without registering a touch. This is the reason that the chestplate must be worn under the jacket. The fencing community sees this advantage as somewhat unsportsmanlike and the use of chestplates by older teens and adult men is sometimes frowned upon, unless done for medical purposes such as for protection of a bruised sternum.

PLASTRON (AKA UNDERARM PROTECTOR) – Worn over the T-shirt, the plastron is a cloth protective device that covers the shoulder, chest and upper arm. The plastron is an important part of the uniform and is required by the rules. Plastrons do not come in lefty and righty versions. If you are left handed simply turn your plastron inside out.

FENCING JACKET – Jackets come in left-handed, right-handed, and ambidextrous styles. The quick way to determine handedness of a jacket is by looking for the zipper. A right-handed jacket will have

Put your leg through the strap BEFORE zipping the jacket!

the zipper on the front left side, away from an opponent's point. A left-handed jacket will have the zipper on the right front side. An ambidextrous jacket will have the zipper in the middle of the back. The weapon arm of the jacket will usually have an extra layer of cloth. A strap (the **CUISSARD**) goes between the legs to keep the jacket from riding up and making a gap between the jacket and the pants. To put the jacket on, you must first step into the jacket where that strap is, and only then put your arms in. An ambidextrous (back zip) jacket will look something like a straightjacket. You will probably need help zipping it up. Ambidextrous jackets are popular with schools and clubs that don't know how many righties and lefties will be in their classes. If you're buying your own, you'll probably go for a front zip. What level of protection should you choose? See the discussion above.

MASK – These protect the face and are therefore masks – try to avoid calling them helmets. They are made with a strong steel mesh that is easy to see through. They are held in place by a wide "tongue" and safety strap in back. They come in various sizes. Pick one that feels a bit snug but does not cause discomfort. You should be able to open your mouth with a mask on. If the mask is loose and rattles around on your head, it might come off while fencing, which would be a major safety hazard. Do not carry masks by the elastic strap on the back because this will cause them to stretch out of shape. Wear the safety strap under the tongue of the mask. When adjusting the tongue, hold it against the top of the mask with your thumb and bend it from that point only.

GLOVE – Only the hand that holds the weapon gets a fencing glove. Gloves are made from various materials and vary in style, but they all have a long cuff that must go halfway up the forearm. The cuff of the glove is worn over the jacket to prevent blades from going up the arm under the sleeve. Most gloves have a split cuff that secures with Velcro and allows for a *body cord* (used in electrical fencing) to attach to the weapon.

FOIL – The foil is one of the three fencing weapons used in modern Olympic style fencing along with the *epee* and *saber*. The foil is a point weapon, meaning you score touches by hitting the opponent's *valid target area* with your foil's point. To put it another way, stabbing = good. Slashing = bad.

Put it another way:
Stabbing = GOOD
Slashing = BAD

The foil blade has four sides, giving it a rectangular cross section. The blade is a maximum of 90 centimeters long – blades for younger fencers may be shorter – and the nonelectric version ends in a flattened dull point that should have a rubber tip on it. Foil blades are light and flexible, and practice foil blades are lighter and more flexible than electric competition blades. The blade flexes so that when you hit your opponent, the blade absorbs the shock of the hit instead of puncturing the opponent. The blade is designed to bend in one direction only, so that the blade arches upwards.

The parts of the practice foil include: (1) rubber tip, (2) steel blade, (3) aluminum guard, (4) leather, felt, or plastic pad behind the guard, (5) handle (also called grip) of some type, and (6) a nut to hold the handle on. If it is a French grip, the nut is called a

Fig. 2. Practice foils: French grip (l) and pistol grip (r).

Fig. 3. Holding the French grip foil.

pommel and helps to balance the foil. If it is an orthopedic grip, there will also be a lock washer as well as a nut.

The blade itself is divided into several sections. The flexible end of the blade is called the *foible*, or weak. The middle of the blade is called the *medium* or *middle*, and the base of the blade near the guard is the *forte* or *strong*. There is also the part of the blade that is inside the handle, which is called the *tang*. The tang of the foil is threaded for the nut that holds the foil together.

Foils come with two basic types of handles, traditional *French* and *orthopedic* or *pistol grips* (see Fig. 2). Both styles have a lefty and righty version, so be sure you specify which one you need. For beginners it is far easier to tell lefty and righty types among pistol grip weapons than it is with French grips, because only the hand for which it is designed can hold the pistol grip comfortably (see Fig. 3). If you look more closely, though, you can tell whether a French foil is right or left-handed by examining it: if you put your thumb on top, near the pad, the handle should curve into your palm near the front and away from it near the back.

Once you know how to hold it properly, please remember that your foil is more like a pen or pencil than a hammer. Use your fingers to hold and manipulate it.

Equipment for competition

You will first need to be a member of the USFA to compete. You can join online, download an application, or even join at the competition venue. Aside from the previously mentioned uniform, you will also be required to have at least 2 electrical foils, 2 foil/saber body cords, and a lame, which is a metallic vest which is worn over the white jacket. Notice that when you buy a new foil it has tape wrapped around the end of the blade. Do not remove that. Electric foils need 15 centimeters of tape to electrically insulate them. Otherwise, your touches may not score!

See the chapter on Electric Foil for a fuller discussion.

6. Warming Up, Stretching, Cooling Down

Even if the class you are attending has no formal warm up period, it is a good idea to do some sort of warm up activity. This may include general exercises such as jump rope, running in place, a game of ball tag, etc. Sometimes the warm up includes fencing-specific motions like advances, retreats, and lunges. The warm-up not only warms the muscles, which makes them more elastic, but it also helps improve reaction speed, so it is quite valuable for fencing. Young children need only a short warm up time, while older adults will need more time to warm up properly.

Once you are warm, stretch. (There's no sense in stretching a cold muscle.) Stretching improves athletic performance by increasing comfort and range of motion and helps prevent certain injuries.

How hard do you need to stretch? Well, you're not a dancer or a gymnast, who need exceptionally strong and flexible bodies and must earn that flexibility through many hours of rigorous stretching. In

Warm up before you stretch. Take the time for a cool-down stretch after fencing.

my opinion, however, fencers probably needn't worry about flexibility beyond a normal healthy range. Footwork practice, including longer and longer lunges from both sides of the body, will improve your flexibility over time. Bear in mind that expert opinion about stretching varies widely and changes rapidly. Your coach may have different ideas.

Stretching should feel good, or, at the absolute worst, produce no more than mild discomfort. It should never be painful.

By all means, stretch all the major muscle groups, including the core, the upper body, and the arms and shoulders. As fencers, though, we need to concentrate on the legs and groin. (The lunge itself is a stretch.) A pre-fencing stretch usually includes slow lunges of various lengths, both left handed and right handed. Your cool-down should also include some stretches.

A cool-down is the reverse of a warm-up. Begin with active but low-impact exercise, then gradually reduce the speed and difficulty until you are breathing comfortably and your heart rate has lowered. Start, for instance, with some lunges, and then do some slow advances and retreats, then stretch, finally a take casual walk around the club while you drink from your water bottle. A proper cool-down will help speed your recovery and help reduce or prevent muscle soreness.

7. Footwork, Distance and Timing

*FOOTWORK is the term used to describe the actions that the fencer uses to move about the fencing strip. The individual actions and distances are listed in the glossary (vocabulary section), so I won't go into them here. Also, I'm not going to explain the mechanics of actions like the lunge. Your coach will do that.

Footwork may be the main focus of a lesson, as well as part of the warm-up period. Footwork is practiced by beginners and advanced fencers alike, and dedication to proper footwork brings positive results. Aside from practicing individual footwork actions, you will practice combinations of actions in order to master useful patterns and develop the ability to use your feet without having to think about them. Once your feet can be set on autopilot, you can more easily focus on your opponent and your bladework. That means more success and fun for you. Occasionally do your footwork drills left handed (assuming you are right handed) to help your muscles develop evenly and to improve your overall coordination.

Do some footwork drills wrong-handed to even out muscle development and improve coordination.

In the beginning you will simply move forward and backward (advancing and retreating) with the goal of maintaining the distance between you and your partner. Quickly, however, you'll begin to use footwork to help you attack your opponent and defend yourself. Your coach will demonstrate and teach the actions. As you progress, you'll discover that you can influence your opponent's actions with your own footwork, which will allow you to better time your attacks and set traps for your opponent.

Footwork is a key element in fencing because it lets you control the distance between you and your opponent. Fencers generally try to stay just far enough away from each other to feel somewhat safe, but close enough to pose something of a threat. If the distance decreases, then the threat of being hit increases.

If the distance is correct, and one fencer *attacks,* a number of things can happen:

• The attack may succeed and the other fencer may be hit (scored upon, or touched);

• The attack may fail because the other fencer actively defends himself: he may retreat out of distance, dodge, or parry (deflect the attacking point);

• The attack may fail because it was poorly executed: the fencer simply misses.

Once attacked, a fencer can use footwork to increase the distance between himself and his opponent. This may be enough to protect him from being hit. If not, the defender may parry. Since he has retreated, he now has more time in which he can parry.

(Time and distance in fencing are analogues of each other. At the same speed, the sword with the greater distance to travel to its target will take more time to reach the target. Distance = Rate multiplied by Time (D = RT). This applies to both footwork and bladework. In the beginning, just remember that if you attack from too far away your opponent will have plenty of time to defend himself.)

Timing your actions properly is another key element in fencing. A good sense of timing, or *tempo* as it is called, is very helpful in fencing. Often musicians and dancers seem to have a bit of an advantage with this when they are learning to fence. Tempo is a very tricky subject and includes elements of distance, velocity, direction of movement, and the opponent's level of awareness. (For more on tempo, see the Glossary.)

Imagine that you are standing near a pendulum that is swinging towards you and then away from you. At its closest point, you can reach out and grab it. When is the best time to reach out and grab it? If you reach out too early you won't be able to reach it and you'll have to wait for it to come to you. If you reach out too late, the pendulum will already be getting away from you. Imagine that the pendulum is now a fencer who is advancing and retreating. It would be best to attack him while he is advanc*ing*, still in motion forward, and entering your reach. You are less likely to be successful if you attack him after an advance, because he is better able to start retreating. Worse than that is attacking him while he is already moving backward.

If you are moving forward at a certain speed and your opponent is retreating at the same or greater speed, you'll never reach him. Learning to accelerate in order to *close the distance* to your opponent is essential. Acceleration is an increase of speed, in this case the speed of your footwork. Remember that it is far easier to accelerate from slow to fast than it is from fast to faster. Not only can you use a burst of speed to reach an opponent, but you can also use changes of speed to influence and trick your opponent. If you advance and retreat at one speed for a while your opponent may get used to that tempo, so then when you accelerate you catch him by surprise.

Vary the speed and rhythm of your footwork to set traps for your opponent.

8. How to Do Paired Drills

The instructor, likely with the help of a partner, will demonstrate a skill for the students to practice. If there is only one coach teaching the class, he will pick a student from the class to help with the demonstration. Don't be afraid of being picked. The person chosen to help demonstrate the drill gets to practice that skill for a longer period of time than the rest of the class and he gets to do it with the coach himself. These are certainly benefits of being selected as the partner for the demonstration. The coach may select his demonstration partner based on several criteria. For example, he may try to pick someone new each time in order to seem fair; or he may want to work with the most experienced or least experienced person; or he may want to demonstrate a skill with an opposite-handed fencer.

If you don't understand, don't be afraid to ask the coach. You are probably not the only one who didn't get it.

When you practice that action repeatedly with a student partner, it is called a paired drill. A drill may focus on a specific action or strategy or it may allow you some freedom to choose what to do depending on the actions of your partner.

While observing the demonstration of the drill, pay attention. Try to determine the following:

(1) At what *distance* does the drill start?

(2) *Do the fencers do any footwork* or are they stationary?

(3) If there is footwork, *who leads it?* How fast is it? (In introductory classes it is usually the coach who leads the footwork.)

(4) *Who initiates the action?* Does the coach cue the student to react? Does the student have the first move?

(5) *What is the cue?* Is the cue a blade action? Is it distance or footwork related?

(6) Is there *more than one* cue? Is there more than one response?

(7) Does the coach stop his footwork to give the cue?

(8) *What is the purpose of the drill?*

After demonstrating the drill the coach will ask if there are any questions. Please, if you don't understand what to do, say so! You might not be alone in your confusion. It is far worse to keep silent and then when you find a partner, to ask, "So, what are we supposed to do?" After all, your partner may not have fully understood either, and even if he did, he may not be able to explain it properly.

Once the questions are done, you will be released to go with your partner and practice the drill. After you find your area of the room to practice, you face your partner and have a little chat with him.

Introduce yourself. Shake hands. Be friendly. Be sure you both understand the drill. Then, and I can't emphasize this enough, *figure out who will take the coaching role and who will be the student.* You'll be expected to swap roles eventually, so you'll both get the opportunity to practice the drill. You don't want to waste any time, so quickly just pick a role and get ready. The rule at my club is, if someone asks, "Do you want to be coach?" and the partner says, "I don't care," then the one who said that he doesn't care is automatically the student. Once you've determined which roles you'll play, salute, put on your masks, and start the drill. After a certain number of actions you'll probably be expected to reverse roles so that both fencers get the opportunity to be the student.

> Agree on who will start out in the coaching role! Then salute — put your masks on — and get started.

Be sure to go smoothly and slowly at first. Once you have been successful several times you can start to build up the speed. Don't get carried away. Fencing is very complex and speed only exacerbates errors. If you are doing well, then wonderful! If you are having some trouble, try to remember just how the drill was demonstrated, start from the beginning, and slow down. Don't be afraid to ask for help.

> Go smoothly and slowly at first. But do the actions realistically.

It is very important that the actions be done as realistically as possible. Consider this drill: both fencers are students, but one is assuming the role of the coach and the other that of the student. The coach attacks and the student takes a parry 4 and direct riposte. The fencer who is coaching may make a short and sluggish attack, one that doesn't even aim at the target, but the student parries it anyway and makes a riposte. Both fencers think the drill is easy, and neither one is feeling very challenged. The student coach is teaching the student to parry something that isn't even a genuine threat.

> Practice realistic actions. Build up to full speed. Threaten the valid target.

This is very bad.

Now consider then the very same drill with a different pair of fencers. The coach launches a quick and well-timed attack. Despite the attempt of the partner to parry, the attack hits! On the next try, the coach makes another excellent attack, but this time the student is better focused and makes a successful parry and riposte. They continue like this and after several minutes they are both deserving of a short rest and drink of water. The student in the coach role was teaching the student to defend against real attacks. The coach was also benefiting because he was practicing his attacks. The student was making real parries and ripostes, and was being challenged to improve.

This is very good.

After everyone is done doing the drill, the coach may ask for volunteers to demonstrate the drill to the class, or he may select individuals to do the demonstration. If you are picked, it may be because you did well during the class, because you did poorly or were just picked at random. Don't be nervous. Just do your best! (*See Figure 4*, Attack and Parry.)

Fig. 4. Attack and Parry

9. Right of Way (ROW)

The term "Right of Way (ROW)" refers to the rules in foil and saber fencing that prevent both fencers from scoring at the same time. If both fencers hit each other at the same time the referee determines which fencer (if any) had the right to score. The rules of ROW are only invoked when both fencers hit. The fencer that has the right to score is the one that initiates the threatening action. If fencer A attacks and fencer B reacts by counterattacking, and they both hit, the referee will say that fencer A had the Right of Way and will award Fencer A the point. Fencer B should have defended himself from the attack so that he may later make his own threatening action. Essentially, by counterattacking, fencer B has chosen murder/suicide, which isn't terribly smart when compared to the option of living to fight another day.

If both fencers hit, only the one with ROW scores.

Neither fencer has ROW at the start. Eventually, one fencer will attack (the initial offensive action) and that will give him the ROW. He will have the ROW until his attack finishes, either by scoring, missing, bending his weapon arm back toward the guard position, or being stopped (parried) by his opponent. If a fencer parries an attack then the attacker has lost the ROW, but the defender doesn't automatically get it. The defender has to establish his own threat to get ROW. If the defender parries and then immediately makes his own offensive action, called a riposte, then he gets the Right of Way because of the riposte. When no one has ROW, the first person to establish a threat gets it.

The rules of ROW also apply when both fencers touch, but the attacker hits his opponent off target. (The target area in foil, roughly speaking, is the whole jacket, front and back, minus the arms. See the diagram on the next page.) The referee will call a halt, as he does whenever there is a touch, valid (on target) or not. If the attack is valid, then he awards a point to the attacker. If the attack is off target then he resets the fencers and then calls "Fence!" to get them fencing again. If fencer A attacks and hits off target while fencer B counterattacks and hits on the valid target area, the referee will call "Halt!" and award no point. The attack, which had Right of Way, was off target.

Now it gets complicated.

What happens if Fencer A attacks, Fencer B parries and ripostes, but Fencer A continues and hits at the same time?

It's Fencer B's touch – *even if Fencer A hit first, as often happens.* Fencer A lost ROW when his attack was parried, and Fencer B gained it by making an immediate riposte. Fencer A could have regained ROW by parrying B's riposte and making his own *counter-riposte.*

You lose ROW by
- "breaking" your attack
- missing or falling short
- being parried

Another way Fencer A can lose ROW is for him to hesitate or withdraw his arm during his attack.

It sounds complicated, and it is. But you will gain a sense of ROW by fencing and watching bouts and trying to understand the referee's decisions.

Incidentally, although Right of Way is often abbreviated in print as "ROW," it is never pronounced as the word "row", as in rowing a boat. It is always referred to as "Right of Way." Also, the term Right of Way does not appear in the official rule book. There it's called "priority."

Epee fencing does not use ROW. Whoever hits first gets the touch, and if both fencers hit at the same time, they are both awarded a point. In addition, the entire body is target, so there are no off-target hits. In saber, non-valid (off-target) hits simply do not count. An off-target hit does not stop the action or prevent a valid hit from counting.

10. Determining Eye Dominance and Aiming

It is helpful for the fencer to know whether the left or the right eye is dominant in order to make aiming easier and more effective. The dominant eye is the eye that sees the same perspective as the person's binocular vision. One way to determine this is to extend both arms and make a small viewing hole between the two hands. Look at a distant object through the peephole and alternate between both eyes open, left eye only open, and right eye only open. The eye that sees the object (the same as with both eyes open) is the dominant eye. Most right-handed people will be right eye dominant. Ideally, eye dominance will match handedness, but this isn't always the case. Determining eye dominance is especially helpful to people whose handedness and eye dominance do not match.

Once the dominant eye has been found, the fencer can improve his ability to aim through visualization. The fencer comes on guard and looks with both eyes at a target. The target should be small and specific: a dime sized spot rather than the whole chest. The fencer extends the weapon arm and relaxes the shoulder. Now he imagines a line being drawn like a laser beam from his dominant eye, along his weapon arm, through the blade, and out the point to the target. Maintaining a relaxed shoulder, he delivers the touch, using only the fingers to make fine corrections to the aim if necessary. The relaxed shoulder allows the trajectory of the straightened weapon arm to remain the same as it was while in the guard position while lunging. To put it another way, the weapon arm does not drop during the lunge. This is all done very slowly at first, but in time the fencer will be able to skip the laser beam visualization and aim and hit at full speed. Eventually the sense of aim will become refined and aiming can be done using peripheral vision.

> Aim at a dime-sized spot, not the whole chest. Imagine a line like a laser beam from your dominant eye to the target.

> **WHERE TO LOOK**
> Students often ask what to watch while fencing — the eyes, the guard, the point? I advise them to look at the opponent's **weapon** shoulder area, which shows the motion of the arm relative to the torso and helps the student judge distance from the torso. Peripheral vision will detect blade movement and foot movement

Fig. 5. Target area in foil (the white area is valid.)

© International Fencing Federation (Fédération Internationalde d'Escrime)

The valid target area includes both front and back of the torso down to the top of the hip bone, plus the collar of the jacket and the groin.– the area covered by the lamé. A new international ruling makes the bib of the mask valid target down to the collarbone, but this rule has not yet been adopted in the US as of this writing. The rest of the bib, the mask, the arms, and the legs are not valid target.

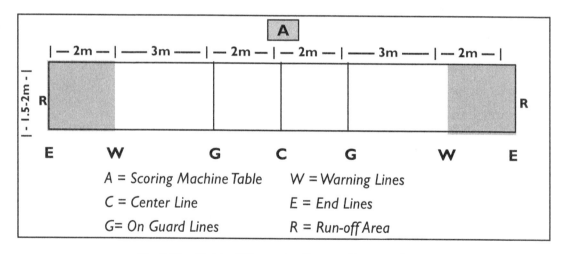

Fig. 6. The Field of Play – the Fencing Piste or Strip

The diagram shows a regulation fencing strip that might be found in many clubs and local competitions. (A championship strip would have a conductive surface that extends beyond the boundaries shown.) Not all strips will have the full regulation width of 1.5m – 2.0, and not all strips will have a full run-off area.

At the start and finish of each bout, and before each new point, the fencers place themselves behind the on guard lines. If a fencer goes off the side of the strip with one foot or both feet, there is a halt, his opponent gains a meter and the fencer must retreat to reestablish correct on guard distance. If he goes beyond the end line with both feet, either while fencing or as a result of a meter penalty, his opponent scores a touch.

11. Your First Bouts

After you learn some actions and do some drills (how many will depend on your instructor), you will fence your first bout. It will be an exciting moment. Remember, though, that your results mean little. How well you do in these first bouts will not determine your later success, or lack of it, in your fencing career. Try to relax and have fun.

A fencing bout takes place on a defined strip, also known as a piste, fourteen meters long and between one and a half and two meters wide – that is, between about 5 and 6 ½ feet. (See the previous page for a diagram of a typical strip.)

Fencing a bout on the strip is governed by certain basic rules. Your coach has probably already explained many of them to you, but just in case, here's a reminder:

- You have to stay inside the strip while fencing – you can only score when you're on the strip.
- You have to face your opponent – you can't turn your back while fencing.
- If one fencer passes another, the referee will call halt.
- You can't grab or push your opponent's blade. You can't protect yourself with your unarmed hand and arm, or cover your target with non-valid target.
- If you and your opponent make contact with each other using anything except your weapons, a halt will be called and one or both of you will be penalized. The weapons can make contact with each other and the points of the foils can strike the opponent. All other contact is illegal in foil.

ON GUARD – READY – FENCE

At the start of each bout, take your position behind your on guard line, mask off. Face your opponent, make eye contact, and salute. Salute the referee if there is one (often, in recreational bouts, there isn't, so you and your opponent will have to make all the calls yourselves.) After saluting, put your mask on and come on guard at the ref's command.

The referee will call, "On guard!" and ask "Ready?" If you're not ready, call out "No, sir (or ma'am.) It's polite to say "Ready, sir," if you are ready, but if the referee hears nothing to the contrary, he will give the command, "Fence!" Again, if there's no referee, each of you has to make sure that the other is ready. Sometimes you will call "Ready? Fence!" aloud; sometimes you can nod or slap your rear leg. Sometimes your coach will give just one of you the responsibility of acting as referee, including calling "Fence!" and keeping score.

When a fencer makes a touch, whether or not it's valid, the referee calls "Halt!" and both fencers must immediately stop. (If there's no ref, the two of you should just stop.) The referee then analyzes the action and determines whether a touch has been scored. If not, the fencers come on guard where the halt was called, making sure that they start far enough apart – a distance so that their extended blades can't touch each other. If a touch has been scored, the fencers return to the on guard lines and the process starts over with the commands "On guard! Ready? Fence!"

SCORING

Each touch that's awarded scores one point. The first fencer to 5 points, or touches, wins a standard bout. (In tournaments, direct elimination or DE bouts can extend to 15 touches.) In competitions and many recreational bouts, there's also a time limit. You'll have a maximum of 3 minutes of actual fencing time (the time between "Fence!" and "Halt!") to score those 5 touches. The clock stops between touches while the referee is awarding points. If neither fencer reaches 5 points when the time runs out then the fencer with the higher score wins.

If the score is tied after 3 minutes – or after the third 3-minute period in a 15-touch bout – the referee flips a coin and awards priority to the winner of the coin toss. Now there is one more minute of sudden death: if a fencer scores, he wins. If neither fencer scores, the winner is fencer with priority.

If you're fencing with an electric scoring machine, it's easy to tell when there's a hit and whether it's valid. If you're fencing "*dry*," it's much harder. It's good sportsmanship, and good for your fencing progress, if you acknowledge possible touches against you. That way the action won't get too confusing. If there's a referee, pay attention to his analysis of the action – you can learn a lot from understanding how your moves look to an outsider. If there's no referee, give some weight to your opponent's opinion.

THINKING ABOUT YOUR FIRST BOUTS

OK. From the command "Fence!" you start fencing the bout. But what is that really? Fencing a bout – bouting – is very different from drilling. In your classes you did drills that let you practice specific techniques and tactics.

Now everything seems different. Drills were cooperative. Fencing bouts are the opposite of cooperative. They are competitive.

In a bout, you are trying to use the skills that you learned in a cooperative drilling environment. But this time, you are trying to defeat your partner – who is now your opponent. You will use your footwork to maintain a fighting distance, close enough to be threatening, but far enough to offer some safety. You will be trying to hit your opponent; your opponent will be trying to avoid your touch and hit you instead. Through continued footwork and bladework, you try to create openings in the opponent's defense or take advantages of his mistakes. You will try to use strategies to increase the odds that your actions will score and to help create new opportunities.

Some people will focus on technique, use only the moves that they know, and will either win or lose. Other people will just go nuts and try to win, not caring whether they are using what they were taught or making up stuff as they go along. Some people are a bit inhibited; others put in an incredible amount of athletic effort. All of these people will either win or lose, but winning or losing is no guarantee of future success for anyone at this stage.

Among inexperienced fencers, previously acquired physical ability does play a big part, but with experience, proper technique starts to kick in. Eventually almost anyone who dedicates himself or herself to the sport will become proficient.

Try not to get carried away. Practice even when you are bouting. When you fence, it is important to try to use the actions that you are taught by your coach. It may seem risky to attack while you are learning attacks or it may seem risky to allow your opponent to attack in order to for you to practice your parries, but it is an important part of the learning process.

Sometimes you may discover an action that worked for you and let you score a point or even beat your opponent. Your coach may congratulate you for stumbling upon a real fencing action that you simply haven't been taught yet. On the other hand, he may reprimand you. It may seem confusing to be told "Don't do that again." after a successful move, but success against another beginner does not guarantee success against better fencers. For instance, jumping up and down aggressively may scare or confuse a beginner, but have no effect against an experienced fencer.

Win or lose, it is very important to be a good sport about it. At the end of the bout take off your mask, salute, and shake hands with your non-weapon hand. (Be sure you don't wipe your sweaty face off with your bare hand before you offer it to shake hands with your opponent.) Thank your opponent for the bout and smile while you do it. It is fine to be a hard-nosed competitor when your mask is on and you are in combat mode, but once the mask comes off, you need to be kind, gracious, and well mannered. Un-sportsmanlike conduct is grounds for a severe penalty. Lose your temper and you will be unwelcome at your club or even get kicked out of a competition!

Thank your opponent for the bout — and smile while you do it!

Whether you are doing a drill or fencing a bout, you should think about the purpose of the action you are doing as well as what your opponent could do to defeat it. No fencing action is unbeatable. There will always be a way for your opponent to overcome the action you may be practicing. Why bother then if there is always a way for your opponent to defeat what you are doing? No person is a perfect fencer. Even very good fencers cannot perform their best 100% of the time. If you ever ask "Well, couldn't the opponent just…?" Then the answer will probably be "Yes he could, but will he?" We practice actions that we hope, if we do them well and at the right time and distance, will work, but we recognize that there is a chance that they will not. Remember too that you will always have an opportunity to defeat the actions done by your opponent as well.

TRAINING BOUTS

Some of your early bouts will be "controlled" bouts or training bouts. Training bouts may emphasize or prohibit the use of specific strategies or actions for one or both fencers. They bridge the gap between drills and competitive fencing because, although they are fairly drill-like, they are scored and a fencer will win. A drill cannot be won.

Here are some examples of training bouts:

1) Attack vs. parry riposte
2) Attack vs. counter attack
3) Attack vs. parry riposte or counter attack
4) Attack vs. attack (Your only defense is footwork: no parries or counterattacks!)
5) Simple attack or compound attack vs. parry riposte
6) Offensive second intention vs. parry riposte
7) Compound attack vs. parry riposte
8) Simple attack vs. full repertoire

9) Counter attack vs. full repertoire

10) Parry-riposte vs. full repertoire

11) 5 pushups each time you score and 5 sit-ups each time you are hit

12) Normal rules, but off-target attacks also subtract a point from the attacker

13) Simple indirect attacks vs. invitation with sweep and parry riposte

14) Full repertoire vs. "Heavy Defense" (Trying to run the clock and not be hit.)

12. Practice at Home

After several weeks of classes you should be able to do footwork well enough that you can get permission from your coach to practice at home. Here are some things you can do at home alone or with the help of a non-fencing partner:

Lunges – Build up to 50 lunges a day to develop strength, flexibility and balance. Be sure to focus on technique rather than speed, and remember that the *recovery* back to the guard position is just as important to do well as the forward motion of the lunge itself.

Footwork patterns – If you have enough room to do so, do laps across the room in various patterns such as:

- Advances to the wall and retreats back
- 2 advances and 1 retreat to the wall, 2 retreats and 1 advance back
- 2 advances 1 retreat lunge with rear recovery to the wall and 2 retreats and advance lunge back
- Random (no pattern) footwork done against an imaginary opponent

If you have someone to help you then you can do drills that allow you to keep distance with him. Have your partner stand in front of you about 10 feet away. Have him walk forward and backward while you do retreats and advances to maintain the distance. Have him occasionally clap his hands to cue you to lunge.

In addition to footwork, you can also practice your bladework even if you don't have your own foil. A simple wooden dowel is an inexpensive and easy to get foil substitute for practicing parry positions etc. at home. Until you have the terminology memorized, you should say aloud the actions that you are practicing. While you do the actions, say aloud "I am coming on guard in parry position 6, which defends the high outside line. I am making a retreat and a parry 4, which defends the high inside line, and now a riposte." Do this for every parry position, the various attacks, footwork, and strategies.

13. Moving Beyond the Beginner Class

After your introductory fencing course, you will probably have a few options to consider. The first is whether or not to continue with fencing. Obviously I'm biased here and I hope you continue. I feel strongly that fencing offers many benefits and is worth doing your whole life. That being said, if you are unable to continue, you can still feel proud that you completed your fencing course and now have a better idea of what fencing is all about. You have, if only for a couple of months, set yourself apart from all those who have thought to themselves that they would like to pick up a sword someday but never have.

If you do continue with fencing (hooray!) then you should talk to your coach about the more advanced classes available to you. You might be able to take classes in more advanced foil, or begin epee or saber. Some clubs offer group classes only for introductory foil and rely on individual lessons for the more advanced instruction. If more advanced instruction is not available to you (perhaps you've taken a class at a local recreation center or community college), then ask your coach or check the USFA website for a fencing club in your area where you can continue fencing. Once you are set to continue with fencing, it would be a good idea to purchase your own equipment.

Ask your coach about clubs, or check the USFA website — www.usfencing.org — to find a club in your area.

If budget is a concern, many fencing equipment vendors sell beginner kits that include just about everything you'd need for basic fencing at a reduced cost. Those sets are good because they are relatively inexpensive and you pay only one shipping fee instead of several shipping fees from ordering the equipment piece by piece. As I mentioned earlier though, buy the best protective equipment you can afford, especially if you are an adult who will not be outgrowing it. If your budget allows, the purchase of good FIE equipment will be well worth it.

Remember when you first came to the club and how amazed you were at what the experienced fencers were doing? They seemed so quick, so skilled; you might have thought, "That's incredible! I could never do that!" Well, if you've been fencing for some months, do they still seem that way to you now? Do you still look at them with wonder? Or perhaps you look at them and think, "That was a great feint attack! I can do that too." Now the next set of beginners comes into the club and sees you practicing. What are they thinking about you? Maybe you are amazing to them! I remember when a beginner complimented one of my students with, "Wow, you're great! I wish I could fence like that." My student hadn't thought of herself as a good fencer, in fact, she thought she was simply dreadful. She had been comparing herself to people who had far more experience than she did. After hearing the compliment, however, she realized how far she had come in the brief time she was fencing. From then on her attitude was far more positive.

If your coach offers individual lessons you should consider taking them, especially if you are interested in entering competitions. Individual lessons are usually twenty to thirty minutes long. Group lessons are usually fine for learning and practicing actions and strategies, but individual lessons are better for improving technique, distance, and timing. In an individual lesson the coach can act as a teacher, partner, or opponent, and can tailor the instruction to best fit the needs of the student. Through the individual lesson the coach and student often forge lifelong relationships built on trust and a mutual love of fencing.

14. Electric Foil

Hamlet: One.
Laertes: No.
Hamlet: Judgment.
Osric: A hit, a very palpable hit.
Hamlet, Act V, Scene II

"I hit you."
"Not with the point, you didn't. It was flat (or too light). And anyway, it was off target: it hit my arm on the way in."
"Did not."
"Did too."
Any fencing club where people are fencing non-electric foil

There are some built-in frustrations in non-electric (dry) foil fencing: Was it a hit or not? And did it land on valid target? Your opponent might not know for sure, or he may even be tempted to be dishonest. It isn't always the word of the opponent you may mistrust, either. In dry foil, you may find yourself wishing that the referee were capable of refereeing with 100% accuracy. Fencing actions can be lightning fast and hard to see. What makes it even more difficult is that touches may occur on areas of the body that are not visible to the referee. The electrical scoring addresses all of these concerns (except the competence of the referee). Most foil fencers greatly prefer to fence electrically when they have the chance. Therefore, sooner or later, you'll be asked to fence electric foil.

These are the parts that make up the system:

SCORING MACHINE; FLOOR CABLES, PLUS CABLE REELS OR PULLEY SYSTEM – In electric fencing, both fencers are connected to a scoring machine (actually a small computer) by means of three-strand wires that move with them

Foil Lamé

as they fence. In most cases, spring-loaded reels pull the wire in during a retreat and let it out during an advance. (Some setups use a bungee and pulley system that accomplishes the same purpose.) The tension of the reel cable is not strong enough to hinder the movement of the fencers. The reels are connected to the scoring machine by floor cables.

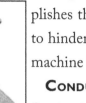

Electric Foil

(2-Prong Socket)

CONDUCTIVE VEST OR LAMÉ – You'll wear the conductive vest over your fencing jacket. Most people call it a lamé, because the material it's made from is usually lamé (a cloth that includes a metallic weave). The lamé defines the valid target area, so there is no more guessing about whether touches are valid or off target. Only hits on the lamé count.

ELECTRIC FOIL, ELECTRIC FOIL POINT, FOIL WIRE – You'll be carrying an electric foil. This has a spring-loaded tip that won't go off until it's depressed – no more flat hits – and won't go off unless it arrives with enough force to depress a spring strong enough to support a 500g. weight – no more arguments about whether the hit was too light. A wire runs down a groove in your foil blade to a socket behind the guard of your foil.

Body Cords

Above: Bayonet

Below: 2-prong

The blade and wire carry the circuit that registers touches. This circuit is normally closed. When the tip is depressed, it breaks the circuit, communicating to the scoring machine that a hit has been made.

BODY CORD – Both your foil and your lamé will be connected to the scoring system by a body cord, which has three wires. Two of them attach to the socket of your foil, run inside your sleeve, up your arm, and out at the bottom of your jacket. Here a plug attaches to a socket at the end of the reel cable. The body cord's third wire attaches to the third post in the plug, clips to your lamé, and thus connects to the reel cable and the scoring machine.

If you look at the three-prong (banana) plug at the back end of your body cord, you'll see that two prongs are close together and one is further away. The close plugs are called A and B (the middle one is B). The far plug is C. In foil, the B and C lines connecting to these plugs and carry the scoring signal, while the A line connects the lamé to the system.

Note: Foil and Saber use the same types of body cords, either 2-prong or bayonet. Epee uses a body cord that has three prongs on each end.

SOCKET – Foil sockets come in a variety of styles and models. Broadly speaking, these are the 2-prong and bayonet styles. Each has advantages and disadvantages. Until you are an experienced fencer with enough equipment to carry lots of spares, choose the style that most of your club prefers. That way, if something goes wrong with your equipment, you can borrow from a friend, and if something goes wrong with a clubmate's equipment, you can share yours.

Hooking up for electric foil

Before putting on your fencing jacket, hold the bayonet or 2-prong end of your body cord in your weapon hand. Then put your fencing jacket on. This will make sure that the wire runs up your sleeve. Make sure that it comes out of your jacket on your weapon hand side. Next, put on the lamé. It's like putting on a fencing jacket, except that there are no sleeves. Step through the strap and make sure that the lamé is on correctly. Now attach the body cord wire with the alligator clip to the back of the lamé. The clip must attach on your weapon hand side. Now plug the three-prong connector of the body cord into the reel cable socket. The socket should have a retaining device to make sure that the plug doesn't fall out accidentally while you're fencing. Use it. Clip the plug to a D-ring that you should find on the back of your lamé or your fencing jacket. Plug the front end of your body cord into the socket behind the guard of your foil (there's only one way to do it). Now you're set to fence.

At this point, the referee will instruct you to test your foils on each other's lamé. Hold your mask in front of your face while you do this. Now return to the on guard line, salute your opponent, salute the referee, and get ready to fence.

When someone touches an opponent's lamé, the scoring machine will buzz and show a red or green light for the fencer making the touch. If the touch is made on anything else (off-target), the scoring machine will buzz and illuminate a white light.

Troubleshooting electric foil

Various problems can show up in the electric foil system, and they will. Armorers and fencing clubs may own testing devices (ohmmeters) that are specially adapted to test body cords and fencing weapons. Their use can greatly speed up the troubleshooting and diagnosis of faulty equipment. They are also often used at the start of competitions to ensure that equipment is working properly in order to avoid delays later in the day. But even after testing, problems can develop.

This section gives some quick and simple ways of dealing with them on the strip. Please note that when the text suggests replacing an item, I don't mean for you to simply throw it out and buy a new one, just that you should set it aside so that it can be repaired at an appropriate time. While fencing, especially at a competition, it is much better just to reach for a spare item than delay the bout by trying to make a repair on the strip.

Here are some common issues in electric foil fencing:

- The machine keeps buzzing and showing a white light, even when no hit is happening
- The machine signals off-target (non-valid) when a good touch is being scored
- The point is depressed, but nothing happens.
- Strange things happen that make no sense at all.

If you're having trouble when you first plug in, make sure that the machine is ON and set on FOIL. Make sure, too, that both you and your opponent have both plugged in both ends of your body cords and that your alligator clips are attached to your lamés, not your fencing jackets.

If a problem comes up after you've started fencing, this is probably the quickest procedure:

1) Switch weapons with your opponent. If the problem switches to the other side, then the weapon is at fault. Check it quickly for quickly-fixable problems (see below). If it can't be fixed quickly, replace it.
2) If the problem doesn't switch sides when you switch weapons, take your weapon back, switch sides with your opponent, and hook up again. If the problem switches sides along with you, then it's your equipment – usually the body cord. Try a different one.
3) If the problem isn't located by switching weapons or having the fencers switch sides, then it isn't with the fencers' equipment, but with the reels and cables behind the fencers. (It's rarely the scoring machine itself.)

Diagnosing Simple Problems

OK, now you've located the problem, switched out the equipment, and you're ready to continue fencing. But what was wrong in the first place? Here are a few hints that can save time and repair costs:

If your off-target light keeps going off, there's an interruption in the touch-signaling circuit (the B-C circuit).

- Check your weapon. Is the barrel of the point screwed on tightly to the blade? Has the handle started to loosen? (These are two problems that can sometimes be repaired quickly on the strip if the right tool is handy.) Is the blade wire broken? Since the tip, blade, guard, and socket are part of the circuit, looseness in the weapon or a break in the wire can cause a break in the circuit.
- If you're plugged in, you can tell if the weapon is faulty by unplugging it and shorting across the ends of the body cord. With a two-prong body cord, you can easily short across the guard; it's just a little trickier with a bayonet-style body cord. (You can also use a key or a screwdriver.)
- If the buzzer stops sounding when you short out the body cord, then the fault was in the weapon. If it keeps sounding, the problem wasn't in the weapon. It is probably it's the body cord.
- If the problem turns out to be your body cord, remember that you can repair it – but not on the strip.

If you get a white light (off target) when you touch your opponent's lamé, the problem is usually (not always):

- Your opponent's lamé isn't clipped, or there's a dead spot in your opponent's lamé (improve the conductivity by cleaning the dead spot, or change the lamé.) A lamé with a small dead spot can be repaired later by sewing on a patch of lamé material.
- There's a break in your opponent's body cord "A" line, connecting his lamé to the reel. Replace the body cord.

If you touch your opponent, on or off target, and get nothing,

- The machine isn't on, or it isn't set to foil. Turn it on. Set it to foil.
- Your weapon is shorting out. Unplug the weapon. If the white light comes on now, replace it.

For problems more complicated than these, consult your coach or the club's armorer. If you like solving problems like these, think about becoming an armorer. If you do, you will always have lots of friends in fencing and may be able to earn a little money making repairs.

15. Competitions and the Referee

Many fencers fence recreationally, meaning that they don't compete except in club bouts, but for many others competition is an important part of their fencing lives. Fencers compete for various reasons and not all of them are associated with the desire to win competitions. Competitions are a way to fence people you don't normally get to fence. If your club is small and you fence the same four people all the time, go out and compete to add variety to your fencing life. Competitions are an important part of the training process. They offer challenges you might not find at your club and will help you to improve your fencing. After a competition you can return to your club with a better awareness of your strengths and weaknesses and can fuel your desire and ability to improve. Tell your coach "My opponent beat me by doing X." Then you and your coach can work on dealing with that technique or strategy. Competitions are good ways to meet new friends (and hit them with swords) and many fencers compete just for the social rewards.

Finally, there is the reality that competitions are also about winning, testing yourself, and trying to prove to yourself that you can be the best at something. A case full of trophies and medals doesn't exactly harm a competitor's self-confidence. If you are part of a high school or college fencing team, competition takes on an added sense of importance because you represent your school and your teammates rely on you to do your best. Competing for a fencing team is especially fun because the team supports its members and cheers for them.

Once you are comfortable with the idea of competing — the winning, the losing, & the stress — by all means look for your first competition.

There is no rule about when you can start competing, but most coaches would suggest waiting till you've fenced for at least six or eight months before entering your first competition, and even then to use it as a learning experience. When it comes to deciding whether or not a fencer is ready to start competing, the proper attitude, I think, is even more important than being able to win bouts at the club. Before entering a competition, a fencer should be comfortable with the idea of competing; with the winning and the losing and the stress that goes along with competition. A fencer who would be emotionally crushed if he competed and lost is not ready to compete. A fencer who has learned the basics, can fence safely, and has a positive attitude whether he wins or loses, is probably ready.

At a competition, the person you will pay the most attention to is the referee.

The referee in fencing is charged with many responsibilities. He is in full control of what happens on the fencing strip. He calls the fencers to the strip when it is their turn to fence. He inspects their equipment for safety, proper fit, and legality. He calls to the fencers to salute, put on their masks, and come on guard. He tells them to start fencing with "Fence!" and tells them to stop fencing with "Halt!" He awards points for valid touches and gives penalties for rule infractions. He (or a scorekeeper and/or timer under his supervision) keeps score and times the bout. He is also supposed to keep the competition running smoothly and quickly, with as few delays as possible. He ensures that neither fencer has an unfair advantage over the other. If you download a copy of the rulebook, you can look through it to find more details about the referee, offenses that can earn penalties, and what the penalties are.

USFA competitions usually follow the same format. The AskFred website (www. ask-fred.net) allows competition organizers to list their competitions and interested fencers to preregister and pay for them. If fencers have preregistered, they check in at the registration desk and show their USFA card. Otherwise, they register and pay at the door. Sometimes there is an extra charge for late registration.

When all the fencers have checked in, the organizers seed the event, dividing the fencers into "pools" of even strength while the fencers warm up. Once the event has been seeded, the host will call the fencers together to tell them which strip to go to. For example, if there are 30 people fencing in the men's foil event, they may be divided into five pools of six fencers. (If there are 31 fencers, there might be 4 pools of 6 and one of 7.) Each fencer fences the others in his pool. The fencers are then ranked by their success in the pools, as shown in the score sheet on the next page.

The fencer with the most victories is ranked first; the one with the next-highest victory total is ranked second, and so on. If there's a tie in number of victories, the fencer with the higher "indicator" is ranked higher (the indicator is the difference between the number of touches scored and the number received – TS - TR.) If there's still a tie, the higher ranking goes to the fencer with the most touches scored. In other words, the number of victories is the most important factor, followed by the TS - TR indicator, followed by the number of touches scored.

Look at the blank pool sheet on the next page, then take a look at the score sheet on the page after that to see how it might be filled out in an actual tournament.

Barrage	#	1	2	3	4	V	TS	TR	Ind
	1	■							
	2		■						
	3			■					
	4				■				

Club	Name	#	1	2	3	4	5	6	7	8	V	TS	TR	Ind	Pl
		1	■												
		2		■											
		3			■										
		4				■									
		5					■								
		6						■							
		7							■						
		8								■					

Warnings: _____

_____

_____

_____

Pool of 4 6 Bouts	Pool of 5 10 Bouts	Pool of 6 15 Bouts	Pool of 7 21 Bouts	Pool of 8 28 Bouts	Special Bout Orders For Teammates			
					Pool of 6	Pool of 6	Pool of 7	Pool of 8
1-4	1-2	1-2 5-3	1-4 5-13-5	2-3 8-33-7	1-4 6-4	3-1 2-5	1-2 6-21-4	2-3 3-68-7
2-3	3-4	4-5 1-6	2-5 4-31-6	1-5 6-74-8	2-5 1-2	4-2 3-6	4-5 3-42-7	7-4 2-85-6
1-3	5-1	2-3 4-2	3-6 6-22-4	7-4 4-22-6	3-6 3-4	1-4 4-5	6-7 7-55-3	6-8 5-43-4
2-4	2-3	5-6 3-6	7-1 5-77-3	6-8 8-13-5	5-1 5-6	2-3 6-2	3-1 1-66-4	1-2 6-18-1
3-4	5-4	3-1 5-1	5-4 3-16-5	1-2 7-51-7	4-2 2-3	5-6 5-1	4-7 4-27-1	7-5 3-75-2
1-2	1-3	6-4 3-4	2-3 4-61-2	3-4 3-64-6	3-1 1-6	1-2 6-4	2-3 7-32-5	4-6 4-86-7
	2-5	2-5 6-2	6-7 7-24-7	5-6 2-88-5	6-2 4-5	3-4 5-3	5-1 5-63-6	1-3 2-68-3
	4-1	1-4		8-7 5-47-2	5-3	1-6		8-5 3-51-5
	3-5			4-1 6-11-3				4-2 4-17-2
	4-2			5-2				1-7
		Same order for 3 teammates 1*2*3, 4*5*6			3 pairs of teammates 1*4, 2*5, 3*6	four teammates 1*2*3*4	3 teammates 1*2*3	3 teammates 1*2*3

© US Fencing Association

Fig.6: A sample score sheet for a pool
© US Fencing Association

Each of the named fencers in the left-hand column fences each of the other fencers in the order given at the bottom of the page. Teammates fence each other before they fence anyone else. The scores are recorded in the appropriate boxes. Each box will be divided into two parts, one to record a V for victory or a D for defeat, and the other part to record the number of touches scored by the fencer in that bout. (That "Barrage" in the upper right is used for a tie-breaker if this pool is the tournament final, which is rare these days.

The columns at the right record the totals:

V = Victories
TS = Touches Scored
TR = Touches Received
Ind = Indicator (TS - TR)
Pl = Placement: 1st, 2nd, 3rd, etc.

Tournament: Hollywood Classic
Competition: Men's Foil
Round: 1   **Pool:** 4   **Strip:** ____
Referee: _____

Barrage	#	1	2	3	4	V	TS	TR	Ind
	1								
	2								
	3								
	4								

Club	Name	#	1	2	3	4	5	6	7	8	V	TS	TR	Ind	Pl
	Basil Rathbone	1		V5	V5	V5	V5	V5			5	25	14	+11	1
	Errol Flynn	2	D4		V5	D4	V5	D4			2	22	22	0	3
	Douglas Fairbanks	3	D3	D4		D3	V5	V5			2	20	23	-3	4
	Tyrone Power	4	D4	V5	V5		V5	V5			4	24	17	+7	2
	Stewart Granger	5	D3	D3	D4	D3		D2			2	15	24	-9	6
	Ronald Colman	6	D0	V5	D4	D2	V4				2	15	21	-6	5
		7													
		8													

Fig. 7: A completed scoresheet for a tournament pool
Scoresheet © US Fencing Association

Basil Rathbone went undefeated in this round with five victories, twenty-five touches scored on his opponents, and only fourteen touches scored upon him. He placed first in this round. Tyrone Power, with four victories, took second place.

Errol Flynn, Douglas Fairbanks, and Ronald Colman tied for victories with two each, but they did not perform equally. Their indicator points (IND) show that Errol Flynn did best amongst them and he took third place, followed by Douglass Fairbanks with fourth, and Ronald Colman with fifth. Stewart Granger had a rough day, and although he scored touches on all of his opponents, he didn't win any bouts and placed last.

Notice that Ronald Colman beat Stewart Granger 4-2. That is because he was leading with that score when the three minute time limit ran out.

This round of fencing was very close. Every touch matters, so getting the best indicator possible is important, even if you end up losing the bout.

After the pool finishes, you may be asked to check and sign your score sheet. Check it carefully. Mistakes happen; scores are entered wrong. The indicator on the score sheet may be incorrect, and once you've signed, it's too late to change.

Check your score carefully before signing the score sheet. Even a small error can affect your seeding in the next round

Your placement in the pools determines your seeding in the next round – or whether you make it to the next round at all. That depends on the format of the competition. Sometimes all the fencers are promoted; sometimes only a certain percentage. In the latter case, if there aren't equal numbers of fencers in each pool, the winning percentage becomes the first indicator.

After the pools, the direct elimination rounds (DE's) begin. They consist of fifteen-touch bouts. In the DE's the winners move on to the next round and the losers are eliminated from the competition. In the first round of DE's, the highest ranked fencers from the first round of pools fence the lowest ranked fencers, so doing well in the pools give you an advantage in the DE's, because theoretically if you have a high seeding, then your first DE bout will be relatively easy. Needless to say, it doesn't always work that way.

The USFA awards letter ratings to fencers who do well in competitions. All fencers start out as "U" for Unclassified. The ratings are E through A, with A being the highest and most difficult to get. Fencers earn ratings in a given weapon, meaning you can be rated a C in foil but Unclassified in saber and epee. If a competition is described as "Unclassified" then only unclassified fencers can compete in it. Those with ratings are forbidden from entering Unclassified competitions. This gives the newer fencers the opportunity to compete without fear of being smashed by more experienced fencers. Likewise a "C and Under" means that fencers with C, D, and E ratings as well as Unclassified fencers may enter. An "Open" competition is one that any fencer, A through Unclassified may enter. Don't confuse this with events that are called "Group E1" or "Group C1." That means that the winner will earn an "E" or a "C" rating. A "D and Under" competition may be rated a "Group C2" event if enough fencers participate. See the ratings chart on the next page for details about what is necessary to get the various ratings and use www.askfred.net to find competitions in your area.

Classification Reference Chart

COMPETITION RATING	MINIMUM NBR COMPETITORS	RATED FENCERS REQUIRED	RATED FENCERS MUST FINISH	CLASSIFICATIONS AWARDED
GROUP E1	6	NONE	N/A	1 → E
GROUP D1 Changed per BOD 7/09	15	4 E's (or higher)	2 E's (or higher) in top 8	1 → D 2-4 → E
GROUP C1	15	2 C's & 2 D's & 2 E's (or higher)	2 C's & 2 D's (or higher) in top 8	1 → C 2-4 → D 5-8 → E
GROUP C2	25	4 D's & 4 E's (or higher)	4 D's (or higher) in top 8	1 → C 2-4 → D 5-8 → E
GROUP C3	64	24 D's & 12 E's (or higher)	4 D's in top 8 & 4 E's (or higher) in top 12	1-4 → C 5-8 → D 9-16 → E
GROUP B1	15	2 B's & 2 C's & 2 D's (or higher)	2 B's & 2 C's (or higher) in top 8	1 → B 2-4 → C 5-6 → D 7-8 → E
GROUP B2	25	2 B's & 2 C's & 2 D's (or higher)	2 B's & 2 C's (or higher) in top 8	1 → B 2-4 → C 5-8 → D 9-12 → E
GROUP B3	64	24 C's & 12 D's (or higher)	4 C's in top 8 & 4 D's (or higher) in top 12	1-4 → B 5-8 → C 9-16 → D 17-32 → E
GROUP A1 Changed per BOD 7/07	15	2 A's & 2 B's & 2 C's (or higher)	2 A's & 2 B's (or higher) in top 8	1 → A 2 → B 3-4 → C 5-6 → D 7-8 → E
GROUP A2	25	2 A's & 2 B's & 2 C's (or higher)	2 A's & 2 B's (or higher) in top 8	1 → A 2-4 → B 5-8 → C 9-10 → D 11-12 → E
GROUP A3	64	24 B's & 12 C's (or higher)	4 B's in top 8 & 4 C's (or higher) in top 12	1-4 → A 5-8 → B 9-16 → C 17-24 → D 25-32 → E
GROUP A4	64	12 A's & 12 B's & 12 C's (or higher)	4 A's in top 8 & 4 B's (or higher) in top 12	1-8 → A 9-16 → B 17-24 → C 25-32 → D 33-48 → E

Division I NAC and National Championships are always Group A4 competitions.
Division I-A National Championships are always at least Group A3 competitions.
Division II NAC and National Championships are always at least Group B3 competitions.
Division III NAC and National Championships are always at least Group C3 competitions.
Changes in classifications are allowed at USFA sanctioned individual competitions that are restricted to Veterans and to Junior fencers.
Division, Section and Regional Youth and Cadet competitions must meet or exceed criteria for C1 to award changes in classification. (BOD, July '02, July 03).
The USFA does permit classification changes at mixed competitions without regard to gender of fencers.

Fig. 8: Classification (Rating) Chart
© US Fencing Association.
Classification criteria change from time to time; this chart is therefore
presented only as an example. Check for yourself!

16. Skill Checklist

Put a check next to each of these terms as you first learn it and then a second check after you have successfully used that skill in a fencing bout, as well as the dates for each. You'll find that some skills can be used successfully in a bout with little practice while other skills require great effort and extensive practice to master.

_____ *On Guard position*

_____ *Advance*

_____ *Retreat*

_____ *Lunge*

_____ *Simple direct attack with thrust*

_____ *Simple direct attack with lunge*

_____ *Disengage*

_____ *Coupé (cutover)*

_____ *Parry 1*

_____ *Parry 2*

_____ *Parry 4*

_____ *Parry 6*

_____ *Parry 7*

_____ *Parry 8*

_____ *Lateral parries*

_____ *Semicircular parries*

_____ *Circular parries*

_____ *Direct riposte*

_____ *Indirect riposte*

_____ *Feint attack*

_____ *Second intention (offensive)*

_____ *Second intention (defensive)*

_____ *Press Attack*

_____ *Press Disengage*

_____ *Beat Attack*

_____ *Beat Feint Attack*

_____ *Bind (Diagonal Transport)*

17. Fencing Vocabulary

This is not a traditional glossary of fencing terms, but rather one designed for the beginning and intermediate fencer. Unlike many other glossaries, the vocabulary here is divided into several categories for easier reference. It also includes more description and advice than you'd find in a glossary. Many fencing terms are descriptive, logical, and should be easy to remember. Some aren't. But much as the math you learn in elementary school is the math you'll use your whole life, many of the terms you find here are the ones that you'll be using throughout your fencing career. NOTE: *Terms marked with an *asterisk are especially important for you to learn.*

Some fencing motions can be described by more than one term. A "coupé" for instance is also known as a "cutover." Sometimes the term to be used depends on the situation. If, for instance, you start in the on guard position and make a lunge without an opponent in front of you, you have simply lunged. If you have an opponent who is standing still, and you lunge, you have attacked. If you lunge at an opponent who is attacking, you have counterattacked. Likewise, if you have no opponent and you quickly move your blade laterally from parry 6 (guard) position to parry 4 position, you have simply moved to parry 4 position. If you have an opponent who is in guard position, and your blade hits his sharply, you have made a beat in 4. If your opponent is making an attack, then your motion is a parry 4.

There's often more than one right way to do things in fencing, and that includes how to define and classify fencing actions and strategies. There used to be several national fencing "schools," including the French, Italian, and Hungarian, which described fencing somewhat differently. There were even some differences within those schools. In actual practice today, the techniques of the various schools have blended into an international style, but the old terminology persists. In the United States, for instance, many coaches use a French-based blend of terms, but many others use different ones.

Rest assured, though, that most of the fencing terms you will hear and use are generally understood by students of the various schools, and that the true purpose of all this, namely the ability to describe and communicate, is rarely hindered by these differences. If all else fails, just pull out a weapon and show what you are trying to say. If a picture is worth a thousand words, a demonstration is worth a thousand pictures.

Figure 9. On guard position.

17.1. On Guard, Footwork and Distance

ON GUARD POSITION

The *ON GUARD POSITION* is the optimum position from which to move forward or backward, to prepare to defend yourself or attack. It is one of the two main fencing positions, along with the lunge position. In the guard position, the non-weapon arm is behind the torso and the weapon is usually held in parry 6 position. Both legs are bent with the front leg and foot pointed forward. The torso is turned so that the chest faces the opponent at an angle, which reduces the apparent size of the target area and moves the weapon shoulder closer to the opponent. See Figure 5.

FOOTWORK

*ADVANCE – A movement forward made from the guard position, which starts with the front foot and ends with the rear foot coming forward, thus putting the fencer back into the on guard position.

HALF-ADVANCE – A forward movement made by an extension of the front leg from the knee. A half-advance can be used to trick the opponent into thinking that you are about to advance, and it plays a part in compound footwork.

DOUBLE ADVANCE – Two smoothly-linked advances done in succession, preferably with acceleration.

*RETREAT – A step backward made from the guard position. It can be done in two similar ways:

1) Lifting the rear foot off the floor with a simultaneous push backward from the front leg, followed by the landing of the rear foot and the bringing back and placement of the front foot, thus returning to the on guard position. With this method the torso is moved backward in the first tempo, which is ideal for combining with a parry against the opponent's offensive action.

2) Reaching backward with the rear foot first and ending with the front foot and torso coming backward, thus returning to the on guard position. Here the torso moves back in the second tempo, and the fencer is better positioned for making a counterattack.

HALF-RETREAT – A backward movement made by an extension of the rear leg from the knee. A half-retreat can be used to trick the opponent into thinking that you are about to retreat, and it plays a part in compound footwork.

DOUBLE RETREAT – Two smoothly-linked retreats done in succession, preferably with acceleration.

*CROSSOVER FORWARD – A forward movement in which the rear foot crosses in front of the front foot, then the front foot crosses forward to resume the on guard position. Heels stay lined up. The crossover forward covers the distance of a double advance.

*CROSSOVER BACKWARD – A backward movement in which the front foot crosses behind the rear foot, then the rear foot crosses backward to resume the on guard position. Heels stay lined up. The crossover backward covers the distance of a double retreat.

Crossovers cover much more distance in one tempo than regular advances and retreats, which is good if you are not at risk of being hit, but can be a disadvantage if done while at risk of being hit. The forward crossover is illegal in saber fencing.

HALF-CROSSOVER, FORWARD OR BACKWARD – Only the first foot moves; the fencer can then return to guard in either direction.

APPEL – A sharp, quick stamp of the front foot on the floor which can be used to emphasize blade actions like feints and false counterattacks as well as to create an extra tempo in the footwork.

INVERSE ADVANCE, INVERSE RETREAT – An advance that begins by bringing the rear foot forward and then the front foot forward; a retreat that begins by bringing the front foot backward and then the rear foot. These can be useful when mixed with regular advances and retreats because they offer the fencer more variety of footwork as he attempts to play with distance and tempo.

*JUMP FORWARD, JUMP BACKWARD – Forward and backward footwork actions in which both feet leave the ground and land at roughly the same time.

*CHECK – A half-step in one direction followed immediately by a jump in the other. A ***FORWARD CHECK** is a half-advance followed by a jump back. It is a sudden change of direction used to get out of danger. A ***BACKWARD CHECK** is a half-step backward followed by a quick step or jump forward. It is used to surprise your opponent.

BALESTRA – An offensive compound footwork action made with a jump forward in which both feet land simultaneously, followed immediately by a lunge. The balestra is no longer used very much in foil.

HALF INVERSE ADVANCE LUNGE, also called **GAINING ON THE LUNGE** or **STEALING DISTANCE –** An offensive compound footwork action consisting of a half inverse advance followed by a lunge. Since the rear foot is the anchor point of the lunge and determines the reach of the completed lunge, the forward placement of the rear foot in this technique delivers the same results as an advance lunge without first moving the torso forward. Properly prepared with a false attack or two made with a lunge, the opponent may not notice the initial forward movement of the rear foot and will react to the attack as if it were simply a lunge. A fencer who defends against this with only a retreat will be caught by surprise when the attack travels the distance of an advance lunge and scores. Think of this as the advance lunge's sneaky evil twin brother. The standard advance lunge can be modified to produce a similar result by bringing the rear foot to the heel of the front foot during the advance portion of the action, thus producing an advance lunge that covers nearly the distance of two advances and a lunge.

COMBINING FOOTWORK WITH BLADEWORK

*THRUST – The thrust is the extension of the weapon arm toward the target with the intention of hitting the opponent. It can be executed from the on guard position or with various footwork, such as the advance, lunge, and advance-lunge. See *Distances.*

With the weapon arm bent while in the on-guard position, it is important that the elbow be pulled in – that is, in front of the hip – to line up with the forearm and hand. If the elbow is exposed in the outside line, it produces a rotation in the bones of the arm when the arm extends. That rotation affects the aim. A poor elbow position will cause the point to drop and pull to the inside during the extension. By placing the elbow in line with the forearm and guard, the correct position is there before the extension is made, so the extension won't affect the aim. Another consideration is that with the elbow in front of the hip, your upper arm covers your valid target.

*LUNGE – A powerful footwork action that is used to deliver a touch to the opponent's target area. It starts with extending the weapon arm, then a kick forward of the front foot, followed by a powerful straightening of the rear leg and throwing back the rear arm. It ends in the lunge position, where the front leg is bent, the front knee above the front ankle, the rear leg straight, both arms straight (one forward and one backward) and both feet flat on the floor. The motion back toward the guard position from the lunge position is called the recovery. See photo on the facing page.

Most fencers beyond the beginner stage can produce a lunge. Many can improve upon their lunges by focusing on some subtle but important parts of the technique. The first is the application of power in the lunge itself. Once the weapon arm has been extended and the front foot is kicked forward, the rear leg is straightened. I ask my students "If I want to lunge this way, then which direction do I apply the power from my rear leg?" Students tend to suggest applying the power in the direction opposite that the lunge is

Figure 10:. Attack With Thrust

Figure 11. Attack With Lunge

directed, i.e., they say to push backwards. Equal and opposite reaction – right, Newton? Well, the thing is that the rear foot is upon the floor. The floor is not behind the fencer, but rather is underneath. The fencer should apply the power from the rear leg directly down and into the floor using the whole of the rear foot. Visualize breaking though the floorboards with the rear foot.

It is important for the weapon arm shoulder to remain relaxed, especially during the lunge. A tight shoulder will force the weapon arm (and therefore the weapon) to drop during the lunge and that ruins the aim. To learn how to relax the shoulder, you should come on guard and extend the weapon arm. Then make the shoulder like water, feeling the arm almost disconnect from the torso. Whatever movement the torso makes, the arm should not be affected. With the arm extended and aimed, jump up and down with the goal of keeping the weapon arm and foil aimed and motionless.

The lunge can be delivered with different timings or rhythms. You are likely to first learn a lunge which strives for maximum speed from start to finish. This is an **EXPLOSIVE LUNGE**. By contrast, you can start forward more slowly and speed up as your point approaches the target. This is an **ACCELERATING LUNGE**. Finally, you can simply lift your front foot off the floor as you move your point and wait for your opponent's reaction. This is a **WAITING LUNGE**.

A more powerful version of the lunge is the **FLYING LUNGE**. This is a very powerful explosive lunge in which both feet are off the floor mid-lunge. The fencer does not try to jump upward. Rather, the force of the extending rear leg launches the fencer from the floor. A flying lunge can cover the distance of an advance lunge but has the advantage of taking only one tempo. A good flying lunge requires athleticism and strength, not just for the launch, but also for a safe and proper landing in the lunge position.

*RECOVERY - The return to the on-guard position from the lunge position is called the recovery. There are three types of recovery: **RECOVERY BACKWARD**, the most common (bringing the front foot back to on-guard), as well as **RECOVERY FORWARD** (bringing the rear foot forward to on-guard) and **CENTRAL RECOVERY** (returning to on-guard by bringing the front foot backward and the rear foot forward at the same time.)

The recovery seems simple enough. Most fencers know to bend the rear knee and then push off the front leg and come back to guard position. It seems that few realize that the front leg isn't solely responsible for the power required bringing the body back to the guard position. Once the front foot is off the floor the front leg can no longer apply power to the floor and it no longer has much to offer towards the goal of recovering backward. The rear foot, however, is still on the floor. By making use of the traction the rear foot has on the floor, the fencer can adduct (pull in) the rear leg while bending the rear knee. This adds to the push received from the front leg and allows the fencer to pull himself back into guard position more smoothly and easily.

ADVANCE-LUNGE - A compound footwork action made by combining an advance and a lunge, done in that order, with no pause between the two.

FLECHE – The fleche is similar to a forward crossover, but it is an *explosive* offensive action usually done at *advance-lunge distance*. Extend the weapon arm, straighten your rear leg to push yourself forward and off balance, straighten the front leg to continue driving yourself forward, and then swing your back foot forward and make a long crossover. The touch should come before your rear foot lands, ending the fleche. Your momentum will generally make you run past your opponent after your rear foot lands. Practice running past on the non-weapon side at first until you get used to the movement. Take care to avoid causing corps-a-corps. The fleche is most common in epee and is illegal in saber. I recommend it only for fencers who have already mastered the basics and have developed the skills necessary to do it well and with control.

*REDOUBLEMENT – A *continuation of attack* made with footwork after an initial attack fails. An example would be lunge (miss) forward recovery, and lunge again.

*DISTANCES

It is important to understand that, with the exception of infighting distance, that distance is dependent on a person's size and flexibility. A tall adult will be able to reach much further with a thrust and with a lunge than a small child could with the same actions. The distances are not listed in alphabetical order, but rather in order of increasing size.

*INFIGHTING DISTANCE - The shortest fencing distance, where the fencers are less than an arm's reach apart. Introductory foil classes frequently train fencers to avoid this distance, but this up close and personal combat distance can happen accidentally – or on purpose if one fencer decides to surprise his opponent with it. Infighting usually leads to unorthodox blade actions and the fencer who is unexpectedly put into infighting distance is at a disadvantage.

*THRUST DISTANCE, also known as ***EXTENSION DISTANCE -** The distance at which the opponent can be hit simply by extending the weapon arm. See photo titled "Thrust." This distance is also sometimes known as **CLOSE DISTANCE.**

*ADVANCE DISTANCE – A subset of the lunge distance; some fencers describe the distance where you can hit with a thrust followed by an advance as "advance distance."

*LUNGE DISTANCE – The distance at which the opponent can be hit with a lunge. This is a longer distance than the thrust distance. Lunge distance is actually a range of distances, because an individual can make lunges of various sizes. See photo "Touch with lunge." This distance is sometimes called **MEDIUM DISTANCE.*

*ADVANCE-LUNGE DISTANCE – The distance requiring one advance plus the lunge (or sometimes, the distance requiring one *or more* advances plus lunge. Like lunge distance, this distance is actually a range because lunges can be made of various sizes. The distance requiring a single advance and lunge is sometimes called ***LONG DISTANCE,** while a distance requiring multiple advances and lunge is sometimes called **OUT OF DISTANCE.**

OUT OF DISTANCE – A correctly executed attack from close distance, middle distance, or long (single advance-lunge) distance has right-of-way over a counterattack begun just after the attacker's arm extends. On the other hand, if the same counterattack is made on an attack with more than one advance preceding the lunge the counterattack has right of way. The attacker was "out of distance."

17.2. Lines of Target and Parry Positions

*LINES OF THE TARGET

All positions described in first person perspective done by a right-handed fencer.

The target area is divided into four areas known as "lines." An open line is one that allows access to target area. The lines are not static like "left chest" or "right belly" but rather are dynamic, depending on the position of the foil. If you were to stand facing your opponent and held your foil's grip to the middle of your torso with the point aimed at the opponent then half of your target area would be above your foil and half below.

THE HIGH INSIDE LINE – IT'S TEMPTING, BUT HARD TO HIT!

The high inside line is the line that is most often attacked. It is the line that fencers get the most practice defending. It is a very easy line to defend from a purely technical perspective, so it is difficult to hit. A simple direct attack can work if the attack is excellent and the opponent is unprepared, but the odds of that happening are significantly lower than 100%. If your opponent is paying attention, a simple direct attack to the high inside line, especially from advance lunge distance, will most likely fail. Try beating, attacking other lines, feinting, setting up traps with footwork, invitations or second intention, It takes effort but will improve your success rate.

Likewise, half would be to the right of your foil and half to the left of it. In this situation all 4 lines would exist. They are (assuming that you are right-handed):

High outside line – target above and to the right of the foil, your upper right chest.

High inside line – target above and to the left of the foil, your upper left chest.

Low outside line – target below and to the right of the foil, your lower right belly.

Low inside line – target below and to the left of the foil, your lower left belly.

The inside lines are within the grasp of your arms.

As I said a moment ago, the lines are dynamic. If you were to hold your foil in your weapon hand and put your hand above your head and point to the ceiling, then none of your target area would be above the guard of your foil, therefore none of your target area is in the high line. All of your target area is in the low line. If your foil is held down near your knees, then your entire target is in the high line. While in the on guard position, with your foil in parry position 6 which defends or closes the high outside line, you only have the other three lines open.

POSITIONS, INVITATIONS, AND PARRIES

The main positions and parries are illustrated in the photos following this section.

A **POSITION** is just that. It's static.

An ***INVITATION** is a position taken to make it difficult for an opponent to attack in one line and "invite" him to attack in another. Generally, it's wider than a *parry position*.

A **PARRY** moves the blade into a position for a defensive purpose – to stop an offensive or counter-offensive action of the opponent's blade. We can also speak of engagements and attacks on the blade in each of the positions. But right now, it's useful to think of them as parry positions. Each parry defends a specific target area (line.) The parries are defined by the blade position (is the tip higher or lower than the hand?), and the hand position. Each line can be defended by two hand positions – one with the palm turned more or less downward or outward, and one with the palm turned upward or inward. Palm down is called "pronated;" palm up is called "supinated." ("Prone" means facing downward; "supine" means facing upward.) In addition, the tip of the blade can be higher or lower than the hand.

4 lines **x** 2 hand positions = 8 parry positions. Some modern coaches add one or two more. In practice, the positions are part of an infinite spectrum, and their use depends on the circumstances. In theory, for teaching purposes, eight is (almost) enough.

POINT IN LINE (PIL)

If your arm is extended (straight), with your point aimed at the valid target area of your opponent so that there's a straight line from your shoulder, through your elbow and hand, and out to the point, then your point is "in line." This is a very important idea in Right of Way (ROW). Point in line has absolute ROW over all subsequent actions. Your opponent must move your blade out of line in order to gain ROW. Under current interpretation of the rules, you can move forward or backward with point in line and still retain ROW. You can use PIL as a defense, turn it into an attack, or just hold it to slow your opponent down.

But there's one other important position to consider. It's not a parry or an invitation. It's called *Point in Line or PIL.* PIL is important for Right of Way, and it's useful for slowing down an opponent who's eager to attack. See the box above for more on PIL.

Now, let's look at the parries. As we'll see, the parries are known by different names. We'll be calling them the simplest way: 1, 2, 3, etc. They also go by names borrowed long ago from French. They will be designated by all the names that your coach is likely to use.

Remember, too, that when we describe – and even illustrate – the positions, we're approximating. If your coach teaches them slightly differently, he's right. For more on parries, *see p. 86.*

MANAGING YOUR PARRIES

When attacked, don't look at the opponent's blade and whack it away as hard as you can, but instead do trust that moving your blade to the correct parry position (and no further) should be sufficient. In foil, blade contact is all that is necessary to make a successful parry, so simply move the blade toward the parry position until blade contact is made, and then you are free to make your riposte. You do not need to push the opponent's blade to the full distance of the parry positions shown in the photos. The defensive ability of several of the parries overlap, meaning that when attacked, there may be more than one parry from which to choose that will successfully defend the target area. A fencer that habitually uses the same one or two parries may find that he is vulnerable to feint attacks. By using a variety of parries, a fencer can make it harder for his opponent to successfully predict his actions and will therefore become a tougher fencer to hit.

PRONATED (PALM DOWN) PARRIES

The pronated parry positions come first because they are older. They developed in the days of dueling, with weapons that were heavier than modern sport weapons. They tend to be stronger, but less accurate, than their supinated cousins. Not all of them are generally taught in beginning foil classes.

PARRY ONE

1 – The first parry position one can make after drawing a blade from a scabbard. In 1, the tip points down, forward, and to the left, hand quite high, with the palm either down or toward the opponent. This parry closes out attacks made to the left half of the chest (high attacks), but is technically a low line parry because it closes off target that is below the guard. This parry is also known as *prime,* pronounced "preem."

PARRY TWO

2 – From 1, the hand moves diagonally downward and to the right. The tip is below the guard, the palm is down. As a parry, this position closes out or defends the low outside line. The blade will be just to the right of the front thigh. Parry 8 also defends the low outside, but 2 is slightly higher and further forward from the body. It is slower but stronger than parry 8. This is a low line parry. It is also known as *second* or *seconde* (pronounced "seCONED."

PARRY THREE

3 – From 2, the hand makes a semicircular sweep upward and clockwise to 3. The tip is above the guard, hand toward pronation, and closes out the high outside line. The blade will be barely to the right of the fencer's chest. As a parry and position, this closes the high outside line. This is the parry position used as the on guard position in modern saber. It is also called *third* or *tierce.*

So far, the parries can be explained as positions taken, one after the other, after drawing the sword from the scabbard. Now things get complicated.

But first, let's look at a pronated position that's almost never taught (at least, by name) in beginner classes.

PARRY FIVE

5 – To move from 3 to 5, the hand moves laterally (sideways) to the left. The tip is above the guard, hand toward pronation, and closes out both the high and low inside line. The blade will be diagonal or nearly horizontal and low, with the hand in front of the groin. This parry is rare in modern foil as a deliberate action. Instead, a fencer may

start a parry four (high inside line), then realize he should be parrying inside low. This parry position is also known as *fifth* or *quinte.*

SUPINATED (PALM UP) PARRIES

1, 2, 3, 5. What happened to 4, you ask? Let's look at the supinated parries. These are lighter and quicker than their pronated cousins, and they allow quicker and more accurate ripostes. That's why they tend to be preferred as the basis of modern technique.

PARRY FOUR

4 – This position and parry guards the high inside line. The tip is above the guard, hand toward supination (thumb at 11 o'clock). The blade will be in front of the left half of the fencer's chest. Traditionally defined as a supinated parry, it may also be done with the hand toward pronation – though, as we saw, this position is also called 5. (Both of these positions are illustrated in the photographs.) Parry 4 is also called *fourth* or *quart*e (pronounced "cart.")

PARRY SIX

6 – The parry position generally used as the on guard position, having replaced 3. It guards the outside high line. The tip is higher than the guard, hand toward supination (thumb at 2 o'clock). The blade will be barely to the right of the fencer's chest. This parry is also called *sixth* or *sixte.*

PARRY SEVEN

7 – This parry guards the low inside line. The tip is below the guard, hand toward supination (thumb at11 o'clock). The blade will be in front of and in line with the rear thigh. This position is also called *seventh* or *septime* (pronounced "sepTEAM.")

PARRY EIGHT

8 – This position and parry defends the low outside line. The tip is below the guard, hand toward supination (thumb at 2 o'clock). The blade will be just to the right of the front thigh. Its execution differs slightly from the parry 2 in that it is somewhat lower and closer to the body. It is faster but weaker than parry 2. It is also known as *eighth* or *octave* (pronounced "ocTAHV.")

STUDY THE PHOTOGRAPHS

The basic parry positions are illustrated in the pages that follow. Study them carefully and practice moving from one position to another. Remember, though, that your coach may teach slightly different positions.

Figure 12. Parry One (First, Prime)

Figure 13. Parry Two (Second, Seconde)

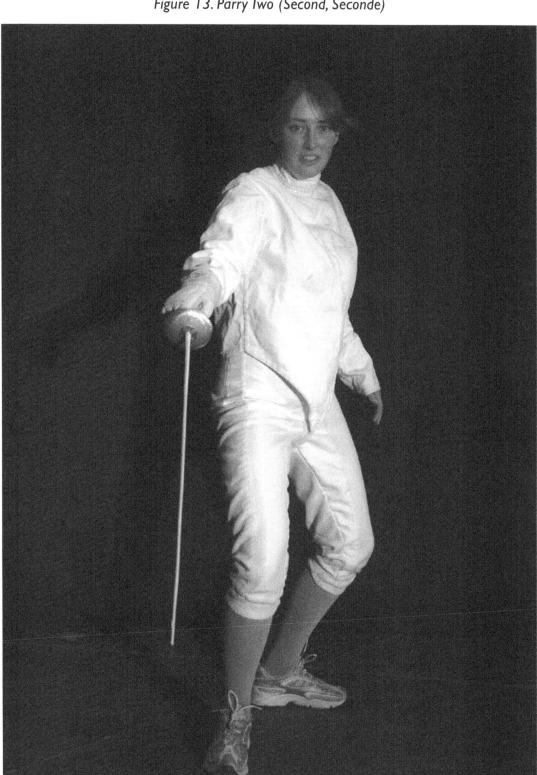

Figure 14. Parry Three (Third, Tierce)

Figure 15. Parry Four (Four (Fourth, Quarte) Taken with Hand in Supination (Nails Up)

Figure 16. Parry Four (Four (Fourth, Quarte), Hand toward Pronation (Nails to the Side)

Figure 17. Parry Five (Fifth, Quinte)

Figure 18. Parry Six (Sixth, Sixte)

Figure 19. Parry Seven (Seventh, Septime)

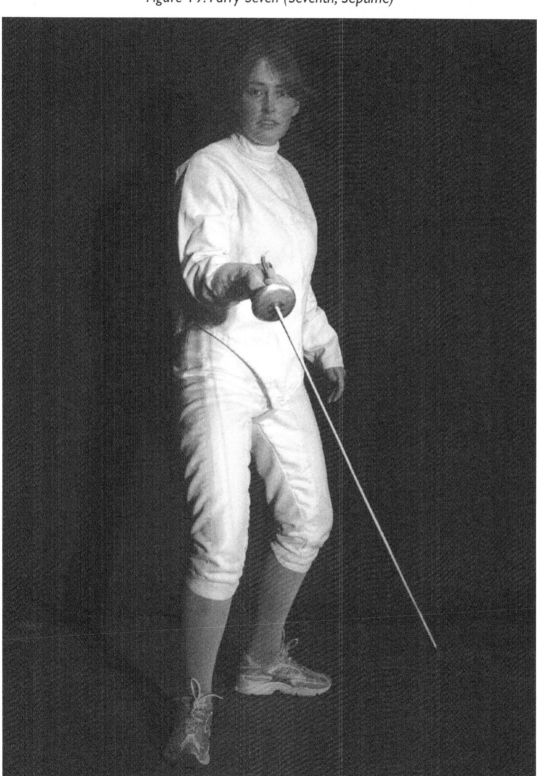

FIGURE 20. PARRY EIGHT (EIGHTH, OCTAVE)

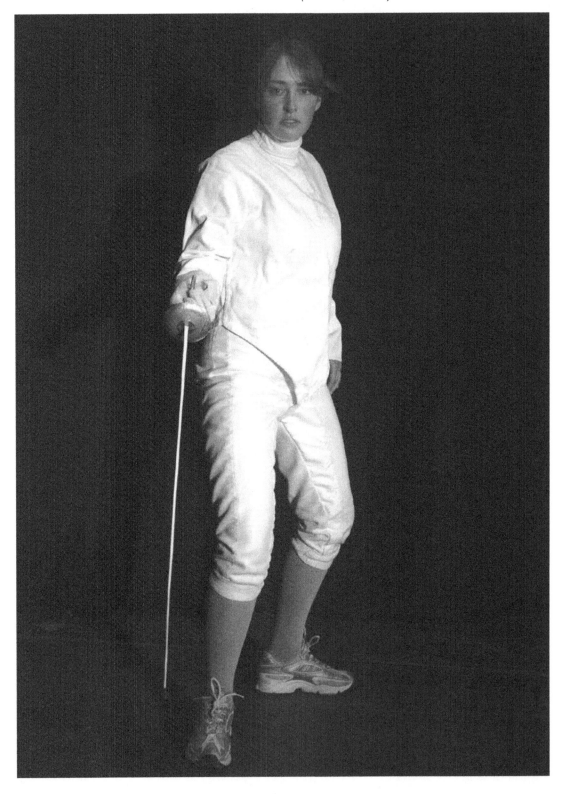

17.3. Bladework

USE OF THE FINGERS

A foil is more like a pen or pencil than a hammer. You should use your fingers – not your arm and shoulder – to control it. Here's how.

It all starts with the choice of handle. For those of you using an orthopedic pistol grip, you need to make sure that the grip you select is small enough to fit into the fingers, not fill the palm, and still be comfortable. For example, I have a very large hand and wear an extra large glove, but I use only a medium pistol grip. Once the proper handle is selected the fingers can be used effectively. Grasp the handle with your thumb on top, slightly bent, pressing down and the first joint of your index finger underneath, pressing upward. These two fingers do most of the work of controlling the blade. They are called the manipulators. The other three fingers rest on the sides of the handle. They are called the aid fingers. The design of the handle will tell you where to put them. Ask your coach to check that you're holding it right.

Holding the foil in 6 position with the hand towards supination (**See p.76**) relax the aid fingers. (Maintain contact with the handle as you relax them.) You'll find that the tip of the blade drops downward somewhat. Now squeeze just the pinky finger and use the index finger as the fulcrum. This pulls the blade to the inside. Finally, squeeze the ring and then the middle fingers. This draws the blade back up to the original 6 position. By practicing this rhythmically, first relaxing the aids then squeezing them from pinky, ring, and then middle finger you can develop a nice tight circle-6 parry. Circle-4 is somewhat trickier because it requires more influence from the manipulators (the thumb and index finger), but the basic principle is the same. Using the fingers to create circular and semi-circular actions help the fencer to make efficient circular parries, disengage attacks, and indirect ripostes. Finger control is also helpful in making strong beats without first winding up. Try it.

WHY DOES MY BLADE BEND THE WRONG WAY?

When you lunge in the high line, the bend of the blade is a test of correct execution. If the blade frequently bends downward instead of upward, something is going wrong and should be corrected. There are a few technical errors (meaning errors in how you are doing your attack) that usually lead to the blade bending downward. If you thrust at the opponent or lunge at the opponent and your tip is higher than your hand when it strikes the target, then the blade will bend the wrong way. First, be sure that at the beginning of your extension that you are using your fingers to lower and aim your point toward the target and that the tip is slightly below your hand at the end of the extension as you hit. If you are lunging, be sure that you are kicking your front foot forward after you begin the extension of your weapon arm. It may happen very rapidly, but an attack with a lunge should start with the motion of the point, then the extension of the arm, and then the kick of the foot. If you start your lunge by leaning your torso forward or kicking first you are far more likely to miss, hit improperly, or even be hit by your opponent with a riposte because you will be telegraphing (showing you are about to lunge before you really do it).

Classical fencers will insist that the weapon arm must be *fully* extended before you kick the foot in the lunge. Modern Olympic-style referees will simply require that the weapon arm *start* extending before you kick the foot.

Even if you extend properly and start the lunge properly, there are still two reasons why the blade may be bending downward.

• First, at the moment of impact you may be bending your wrist by pushing your thumb forward and down. Avoid this by keeping your wrist straight and pushing slightly upward as you hit.

• Second, your front shoulder may be dropping below the rear shoulder as you hit the target, carrying your arm and your blade down with it. Avoid this by keeping your shoulders at an even height, parallel with the floor, even if you allow your torso to lean forward in your lunge.

Blade actions such as the various *attacks* can be made with a variety of footwork. You can make a disengage attack, for instance, with a lunge, advance lunge, advance, a small hop, a giant leap, or no footwork at all.

17.4. Fencing Actions

A fencing action is a unit of movement as defined by the rules of fencing. Actions can be *offensive*, *defensive*, *counteroffensive* (*offensive-defensive* in the rulebook), or preparatory *(preparation)*. The offensive actions are the *attacks* plus the *ripostes* and *counter-ripostes*.

The defensive actions are the *parries*, *defense by distance* (retreating to make the attack fall short), and *evasions* or *displacements* (ducking, twisting, or dodging).

The counteroffensive actions – the *counterattacks* – are generally the same as the offensive actions except for their timing (We'll see some exceptions in a moment.)

There are several types of counterattacks. Counterattacks are initiated after the start of the opponent's attack or riposte and are usually done *in response* to the opponent's action. Sometimes, though, both fencers believe that they are attacking, and the referee will determine, if possible, who had the *ROW* and the attack, and who was making the counterattack.

The *remise*, which is classified as a **continuation of an attack, is** an example of a counterattack that is *not* similar to an attack. It is also an example of how classification can overlap depending on the situation,

• A remise against an opponent who is making an *immediate* riposte is essentially a counterattack and does not have *ROW*

• A remise against an opponent making a *delayed* riposte is essentially an **attack in preparation** and has *ROW*

• A remise against an opponent who is *not* riposting is essentially a new attack.

Preparations set up the offensive, defensive, and counteroffensive actions that you are attempting to use. They include maneuvering on the strip with various footwork, body language, false actions (false attacks, false parries, false counterattacks), as well as the various **attacks on the blade.**

We will consider actions in the following order:
• *Attacks and Preparations*
• *Parries and Ripostes*
• *Continuations of the Attack*
• *Counterattacks*
• *Fencing Strategy and Tactics*
The chapter concludes with an alphabetical list of fencing terms.

ATTACKS AND PREPARATIONS

ATTACK – An attack is an action designed to hit. The rules define it as "the initial offensive action made by extending the arm and continuously threatening the opponent's target, preceding the launching of the lunge or flèche." A *correctly executed* attack has Right of Way over any **counterattack** and must be parried or avoided. Only **point in line** has priority over a correctly executed attack; that is, one made "when the extending of the arm, the point threatening the valid target, precedes the initiation of the lunge or the flèche."

Attacks can be *SIMPLE ATTACKS – made with a single movement of the blade – or *compound attacks (feint attacks)* (attacks in which the final thrust is preceded by one or more *feints*. They can be *direct* (finishing in the same *line* they start in) or *indirect* (finishing in a different line).

*Preparation – A fencer may be setting up an attack for two whole minutes, but in practice, what's usually called the preparation consists only of the one or two moves, designed to finish with an attack, by the fencer with the initiative. (Some people refer to *everything* prior to the actual attack as preparation.) Preparations can be made with footwork or bladework. Any actions with the blade that are not followed immediately by a *thrust* are considered preparations and are vulnerable to an *attack in preparation*.

1. Simple Attacks

A simple attack takes one *tempo,* that is, one unit of fencing time. There are three simple attacks:

*Direct Thrust – A straight thrust, one that finishes in the same line it starts in.

There are two simple indirect attacks. These take one tempo to execute, but finish in a different line. They are the disengage attack and the coupé attack. They must be distinguished from two preparations, the change of line and the change of engagement.

*Change of Line, Change of Engagement – A ***change of line** moves the fencer's own blade from one line to another – from high to low or vice versa, or from inside to outside and vice versa. A change of line by itself is a preparation, not an attack. When it ends by contacting the opponent's blade, it is also called a **change of engagement.** As with all blade movements, a disengage not followed immediately by a thrust is a *preparation*.

Some fencers call a lateral change of line a disengage and a vertical change of line a half-disengage.

*Disengage Attack, Disengage-Thrust – A disengage attack is an attack made with a change of line that moves one's blade around the opponent's *guard*. A disengage against the opponent's blade in high line goes under the opponent's guard; a disengage made against a blade in a low line position goes over the opponent's guard, moving the point forward in one smooth and continuous action, like a corkscrew, in order to hit the opponent in a line different from the line that one started in.

The disengage-thrust is extremely common and effective. It is often the response to the opponent's sweeping blade action. Be sure to make your disengages small, quick, and efficient to increase their chance of success.

*Coupé Attack, Coupé-thrust, Flick – The coupé attack contrasts with the *disengage*. It is a change of line attack made by moving one's blade around the opponent's *point*. A coupé made against a blade in a high line will go over the opponent's point; a coupé against a low line position will go under. The change of line is followed immediately by a thrust aimed at a line different from the line that one started in.

A properly done coupé can hit in two ways, with a thrust, or with a flicking or whipping action. This second action is generally called a flick. It is executed as the downward movement of a coupé-like action, keeping the wrist and elbow loose, then stopping the blade in mid-air – something like snapping a towel or fly casting. The result is that instead of slashing, the blade bends in the air and the point angles into the target.

The flick is difficult to do with the current timing system in electrical foil, but is still possible. You may need a couple of years of experience, as well as sufficient strength, before doing it well. Properly done though, the coupé with flick has two advantages. The first is that it can be very difficult to parry and may require the defender to use both distance and a shielding parry, such as parry position one, to protect himself. The second advantage is that coupés ending with a flick can hit target area that is usually harder to hit with a straight thrust, such as the tops of the shoulders and the side of the flank.

A coupé movement not followed immediately by a thrust is a preparation, not an attack.

2. *COMPOUND ATTACKS

Compound attacks are executed in more than one movement of the blade. They consist of one or more feints – deceptive movements of the blade that seem threatening, but are actually intended to make the opponent parry – and the **FINAL, OR *GENUINE ACTION** – the movement actually designed to hit.

COMMON COMPOUND ATTACKS

*FEINT – An imitation attack, designed to draw a parry or to discover the opponent's reaction.

*FEINT-DISENGAGE – A feint of a straight thrust followed by a disengage thrust into the line opened by the opponent's parry.

*ONE-TWO – A feint of a disengage attack followed by second disengage attack in a different direction in order to avoid a lateral parry and score a touch. In the high line, the point traces a V in one direction, then a V in the opposite direction.

DOUBLÉ – A feint of a disengage attack followed by a second disengage attack which avoids a circular parry. In the high line, the point traces a V in one direction, then another V in the same direction. Compare the one-two.

As noted, any of these attacks can be done with various combinations of footwork. They can be *prepared* by various *attacks on the blade,* including *beats, presses,* and *expulsions.*

3. Preparations and Attacks on the Blade

*Preparation – Preparations are actions of the hand or feet that directly precede the motion of the point or arm that really begins the attack. Although we usually hear of preparations for attack, one can also use defensive preparations, such as a false parry or a false counterattack. One kind of offensive preparation consists of multiple advances down the strip ("marching"). Another kind consists of real or attempted *attacks on the blade.* Preparations are not attacks and do not give right of way. If you are attacked while preparing, your opponent's attack has right of way.

*Engagement – Blade contact. (Think of how gears engage each other to remember this.) Engagement is described by the opponent's blade positions. A pair of right-handed opponents can engage in 4, in 6, etc. A righty against a lefty may be engaged in 6, while his left-handed opponent is engaged in 4.

Preparations on the Blade

These actions on the opponent's blade are preparations. They may be followed by other preparatory actions, or by direct or indirect thrusts. In order to have right of way, they must be accompanied by an immediate thrust.

*Attack on the Blade – These are actions that create blade contact. There are three of them: the beat, the press, and the expulsion. The beat and the press involve contact between the blades near the center of percussion (the "sweet spot" of the blade, about three-quarters of the way toward the point); the expulsion involves sliding contact along the whole length of the blade. They can be executed effectively against an extended or a bent arm.

> ***Beat** – An *attack on the blade* consisting of a sharp striking action against the opponent's blade. The beat itself does not give the fencer the right of way. It can be light or powerful, depending on its purpose, but it makes a single, momentary contact. The beat can be made for several reasons, including 1) opening up the target area of the opponent, 2) learning how the opponent reacts, and 3) provoking an expected response from the opponent. The beat is the most common preparations among beginning fencers.

*Press – An attack on the blade, consisting of a subtle engagement with pressure. It is usually used either to move the opponent's blade out of the way in order to follow up with an attack or to provoke a reaction from the opponent.

Expulsion (Froissement) – An attack on the blade by strong, sudden, continuous pressure, sliding along the opponent's blade. This action is rarely seen in modern foil fencing.

Prise de Fer, *Transport (Taking the Blade) – A *taking (prise)* of the opponent's blade, made by simultaneously engaging and putting pressure on the opponent's blade, controlling it while carrying it into a new line. The prises de fer require longer contact than the attacks on the blade, but they offer more control of the opponent's blade. They are most effective against a straight or extending arm – especially against a point in line or after parrying an attack. A prise de fer is sometimes called a "take," and sometimes a *transfer* or *transport,* because it takes or transports the opponent's blade from one line to another. It's pronounced "preez da fare." There are four: the opposition which is a lateral transport; the bind (1), which is a diagonal transport; the croisé, which is a vertical transport; and the envelopment, which is a circular transport.

Like the attacks on the blade, the prises de fer are preparations that may be followed by other preparations or by a direct or indirect thrust.

*Opposition – An offensive action prepared with a *bind (2)*, a pressure that takes the opponents blade out of line and follows with a thrust while maintaining contact. For example, an attack in 6 opposition takes the opponent's blade into one's 6 position, then maintains the 6 position while thrusting. The idea behind opposition is to ensure that you are not hit while hitting your opponent.

THE BEAT HAS ITS DOWNSIDE!

Beginners overuse the beat, but it has its dangers. It will often alert or alarm the opponent that an attack is about to follow, and can prime his defensive response. This can be a disadvantage for your own *simple attack* following a beat, but can be an advantage for you if you follow plans 2) and 3) above. If you beat your opponent's blade and find out that he makes an immediate *parry*, you can make a beat, then *feint* (fake) a simple straight attack, and finally then *deceive* the opponent's parry with a *disengage* and finish with a thrust into the opening line.

*BIND - (1) In French-based terminology, a diagonal *transport* of the opponent's blade from high line parry position to the diagonally opposite low line – for example, from parry 4 position to parry 8 position or vice versa. The bind (1) is one of the *prise de fer* attacks. This bind is a **DIAGONAL TRANSPORT.**

BIND – (2), in Italian, and generally, in Hungarian, German, and Eastern European usage, a pressure on the opponent's blade that takes it out of line. The binds are named after the positions in which they are executed: fourth, sixth, etc.

CROISÉ – A *prise de fer* that moves the opponent's blade from high line to low line on the same side or from low line to high line on the same side, and finishing with a thrust. Also called a *semibind* or a **SEMICIRCULAR TRANSPORT.**

ENVELOPMENT – A **CIRCULAR TRANSPORT** of the blade that begins by *taking* the opponent's blade in one position, then brings it around with a circular motion to the same position.

TAKE, TAKING – See *Prise de fer.*

*SWEEP – A broad lateral, circular, or other motion of the blade toward the opponent's blade, usually done to find (contact or *take*) the opponent's blade or provoke a reaction from the opponent. A sweep can be done as an invitation to provoke the opponent to make an indirect attack such as a *disengage* or *coupé*. This can be an offensive or defensive preparation.

PARRIES AND RIPOSTES

*PARRY – A defensive action of the blade that stops an offensive or counter-offensive action, generally by deflecting the opponent's blade rather than "blocking" it. The parry positions are named by number for the sake of simplicity. Some schools of fencing list 8 parry positions, while others list 9. The most common parry positions in basic foil fencing are 1, 2, 4, 6, 7, and 8, although 3 and 5 are also described and illustrated in this book. The parry positions are defined by the blade position, the hand position and the target area they defend. See the illustrations and discussion in the previous section. Parries can be *lateral, circular, semicircular,* or *diagonal,* and even, in one case, *vertical.*

*LATERAL PARRY – A lateral (sideways) motion of the blade to a parry position in order to stop the opponent's threatening blade: 6 to 4 or vice versa, 7 to 8 or vice versa.

*CIRCULAR PARRY – A parry that follows a "circular" (actually elliptical, or even V-shaped) motion of the blade, moving from a given parry position around to the same position, taking the opponent's blade in the opposite direction from a lateral parry.

SEMICIRCULAR PARRY – A parry that follows a "semicircular" path (like a parenthesis) from high to low, or vice versa: 6 to 8 and vice versa, 4 to 7 and vice versa.

DIAGONAL PARRY – A parry that moves from a high line position to a diagonally opposite low line position or vice versa: 6 to 7 and vice versa, 4 to 8 and vice versa.

SHIELDING PARRY – A parry taken to *block* (rather than deflect) a *coupé* or *flick* attack. They work like saber parries, intercepting hits that come in at an angle rather than straight on. One version is sometimes called **DEMI-CERCLE, RAISED 7 OR HIGH 7**, but the position taken need not resemble 7. The blade may be roughly parallel to the ground or with the tip slightly raised. The movement is semicircular from 6 or 8 and diagonal from 4 or 7. The pronated parries – 1, 2, 3, 5, and *saber 5* – are effective as shielding parries.

YIELDING PARRY – A parry that makes use of the opposing fencer's force at the point of blade contact and diverts the opposing blade at that point without losing contact. A yielding parry of one is useful against the *prise de fer* in six as well as parry six riposte with engagement. A yielding parry of 4 is useful against the opponent's bind from four to eight (or bind from four to two).

BEAT PARRY – A parry that is made with a beat-like action, bouncing sharply off the opponent's blade.

PARRY OF ENGAGEMENT, HOLDING PARRY – A parry that engages and momentarily maintains engagement with the opponent's blade in order to deflect the opponent's threatening point. It is mostly used against attacks from longer distance and can lead to a riposte made with a bind or croisé. It is more common in epee than in foil.

INTERCEPTING PARRY – A parry that intercepts –breaks into – the opponent's indirect attack rather than deflecting its intended final thrust. It moves the parrying blade directly into the way of the indirect attack. Intercepting parries are usually semicircular. For instance: The blades are both in the line of six. The attacker attempts to disengage into the high inside line. The defender catches the attacking blade mid disengage with an intercepting parry of eight and ripostes.

See p. 67 for how to manage your parries.

MANAGING YOUR RIPOSTES

The *RIPOSTE is an offensive action taken immediately after one's parry. The word means "reply:" it is the answer to the attack. A *COUNTER-RIPOSTe is the immediate answer to a riposte or a counter-riposte. After the first riposte, a series of counter-ripostes can go on indefinitely.

For many beginners, the first problem is to remember to riposte at all, as if just stopping the opponent's attack was the end of things. The solution: practice, practice, practice. But practice correctly.

The next problem is riposting with such a jerky action that you miss. If you have learned to take your parry in the correct position – and especially, not too big – you are on your way. Then, leading with a small motion of the point, you can push your hand straight forward in an accurate riposte.

There are several ways to deliver your riposte, and you should know and practice all of them;

• You can riposte immediately, or you can hold your riposte for a fraction of a second – an eye-blink – to look for where your opponent is most vulnerable.

• You can riposte with *opposition*, *bind,* or *croisé* (maintaining contact with your opponent's blade); or you can make a **DETACHED RIPOSTE**, moving your blade away from your opponent's to make his parry more difficult.

CONTINUATIONS OF THE ATTACK

If your attack fails, but the opponent does not take the initiative immediately, you can consider one of these continuations of the attack.

REDOUBLEMENT – A continuation of the attack made with footwork after the initial attack fails to reach the target. An example would be attack with a *lunge* (miss) *forward recovery*, and lunge again. The redoublement will have *ROW* only if it begins before the defender has begun his own attack. Also called a **RENEWED ATTACK.**

*REMISE – A direct continuation of the attack, made in the same line as the initial attack. It has *ROW* when the opponent parries but does not immediately riposte. Should the opponent begin his riposte before your remise, his riposte will have right of way and your opponent will be awarded the touch if you both hit.

*REPRISE – An indirect continuation of the attack made in a different line than the initial attack. It has *ROW* if the opponent parries but does not immediately riposte.

Should the opponent begin his riposte before your reprise, his riposte will have right of way and your opponent will be awarded the touch if you both hit.

Many fencers do not distinguish between the remise and the reprise. It should be noted that the rulebook gives different definitions of all these actions than those given here. See the vocabulary section for more details.

*COUNTEROFFENSIVE ACTIONS

Instead of *defending with distance*, *evasions,* or *parries,* a fencer can choose to attack the attacker.

You can:

• Seize a moment when your opponent is preparing the attack; (*attack in preparation*)

• Attack during one of the *feints* of a *compound attack* or before the start of the *final* movement of an attack begun with bent arm. In practice, these two ideas tend to merge into one another *(stop thrust, counterattack in time)*

• Attack the *final* movement of a correctly executed attack *(counterattack)*

You can score with a counterattack if your opponent misses. There are counterattacks designed to make your opponent miss and let you score. There are also counterattacks designed to deflect your opponent's attack and score at the same time *(time thrusts, stop hits with steel, stop hits with opposition).*

If you counterattack *out of time* and you both hit, the attacker has *ROW.*

STOP THRUSTS, STOP HITS – A counteroffensive action designed to arrive one unit of *fencing time* before the opponent's attack arrives; that is, on his preparation or on his feints. You can *disengage* away from the opponent's attempt to *take* your blade and immediately thrust; this is a *derobement.* You can stop thrust during your opponent's marching attack with a bent arm or during a lunge that begins with the foot rather than the arm. If you know that your opponent attacks in these ways, it is easy to set up stop thrusts: your extension must simply begin before your opponent's. On the other hand, if your opponent is making a correct feint attack, your stop thrust must *arrive* during one of his feints. Stop thrusts are sometimes called **ARRESTS.**

TIME THRUSTS, TIME HITS, STOP THRUSTS WITH THE BLADE – These *counterattacks* are designed to prevent the attacker from scoring by *closing the line* in which the opponent is trying to hit. For example, if you think that your opponent is going to finish in 4, (high inside), you can extend, while trying to touch, in position 4. (You close the line while extending.)

17.5. Strategy and Tactics

In fencing, the terms "tactics" and "strategy" tend to merge into each other. They refer to plans of action. Strategies tend to be higher-level and longer-term than tactics.

The most complicated strategies require a fine sense of timing, acceleration, and the ability to make crisp and clean actions. They may also require the opponent to do the same. They are presented here because, though they may be difficult for a beginner to *perform*, they are fairly easy to *understand*.

*TACTICAL WHEEL – A diagram in the form of a circle listing strategies (or tactics). Each strategy defeats the strategy that precedes it. The following 6 strategies make up the tactical wheel.

1) SIMPLE ATTACK – An attack that is done with one motion and in one tempo. There are three, which are the *Simple Direct Attack*, the *Disengage,* and the *Coupé*. The simple attack is answered by

2) PARRY-RIPOSTE – A defensive action made with the blade and the offensive action that immediately follows. It may be direct or indirect. It may be simple or compound (feint).

The parry-riposte against a simple attack can be answered by

3) FEINT ATTACK – A false attack done to provoke the opponent to parry, (ideally to make a specific and predicted parry), so that the attacker can then avoid the parry and strike in an opening line. (Note that **SECOND INTENTION** attacks and *Feint attacks* are both used against opponents who are having success with their parries against simple *first intention attacks*.)

The feint attack can be answered, in turn, by

4) COUNTERATTACK – An offensive action that starts after the opponent initiates his own offensive action. In foil, the counterattack is only awarded the point if the attack misses or is parried, or when done *in time* against the opponent's *feint attack*. Counterattacks are far more common and successful in epee fencing than in foil.

Counterattacks can be answered by

5) **COUNTERTIME** – Any action done against a counterattack. Countertime can be done either spontaneously or premeditated as a form of second intention. In foil it is usually done when the counterattacker is hard to hit and you can't rely on the rules of right of way to ensure your safety as the attacker. An example of countertime would be: Fencer A Attacks; Fencer B Counterattacks; Fencer A changes from attacking to

Figure 21. The Tactical Wheel

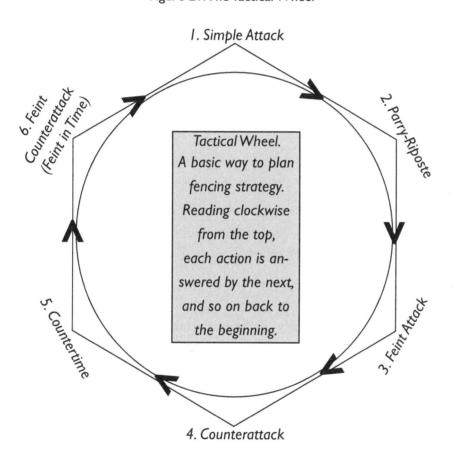

*Tactical Wheel.
A basic way to plan
fencing strategy.
Reading clockwise
from the top,
each action is an-
swered by the next,
and so on back to
the beginning.*

1. Simple Attack
2. Parry-Riposte
3. Feint Attack
4. Counterattack
5. Countertime
6. Feint Counterattack (Feint in Time)

making a parry riposte. *Countertime is a more advanced strategy and may or may not be mentioned in your Introductory Foil class.*

6) **FEINT IN TIME (FEINT COUNTERATTACK)** – A feint of a counterattack done against the opponent's countertime. An example would be: Fencer A attacks; Fencer B pretends to (feints) counterattack; Fencer A tries to parry the feinted counterattack; Fencer B deceives the parry and scores. *Feint in Time is a more advanced strategy and may or may not be mentioned in your Introductory Foil class.*

7) **SIMPLE ATTACK** – the feint in time, of course, is countered by the opponent's simple attack, and the tactical wheel has come full circle.

Other Tactical Concepts

The following tactical concepts are also widely used:

*FIRST INTENTION (OFFENSIVE) – An attack done with the intention of scoring during that action.

INVITATION – A trap set for your opponent made by *opening a line* of your own target, luring the opponent into a simple attack in order to make your own parry and riposte. This can be done simply by moving the blade to a different parry position or by lowering the blade. It must be done in a subtle manner so as to not alert the opponent that it is a trap. An invitation can also be done with a *sweep* which may provoke your opponent to make a *disengage* or *coupé*. The usual method of countering an invitation is to make a *feint attack.*

CHANGING THE TARGET - This strategy can and should be used in combination with other strategies. Repeatedly threaten a certain line of target in order to create paranoia in the opponent about that target area, then feint to that area and attack a different target. This strategy is used during your preparation.

CHANGING THE TEMPO – This strategy can and should be used in combination with other strategies. It simply means that you fence at one speed, or tempo, in order to get your opponent used to that, and then at a critical moment, attack at a different speed (usually – but not always – faster) in order to surprise the opponent.

SECOND INTENTION (DEFENSIVE) – The fencer intends to defend himself not with the initial defensive action but with a secondary one. For example, the fencer makes an initial parry or sweep, expecting that the opponent will deceive it. He then makes a second parry (with acceleration) to deflect or capture the opponent's threatening blade. If the opponent responds to the initial sweep with an indirect attack, this strategy can be described as a form of invitation.

SECOND INTENTION (OFFENSIVE) – The fencer intends to score not with the initial offensive action but with a secondary one. An example would be a *false attack* – perhaps a little bit short – which is meant to provoke a successful parry and riposte so that the attacker can then parry and score with a *counter-riposte*. Note that Second Intention attacks and Feint attacks are both used against opponents who are having success with their parries against *first intention attacks*.

SECOND INTENTION ("OPEN-EYES") – This form of second intention applies when the fencer does not know what his opponent's reaction will be, but makes his preparatory move mentally prepared for any of his opponent's likely responses. For example, the fencer makes a false attack of *feint-disengage* with *advance-lunge*. He does not know whether the opponent will attempt to *parry, counterattack,* or *defend by distance,* so he makes his attack "with his eyes open," ready to take advantage of all possibilities. Open-eyes actions are very slightly slower than preplanned actions because more choices are involved. However, they can be used to great advantage by a fencer with a strong *sense of tempo* – the feeling for the exact moment to attack.

FALSE ATTACK – An attack meant to draw a response or information from the opponent rather than score a touch. For example, a false attack or two may be used to prepare for a feint attack. The initial attack in *offensive second intention* is a false attack.

FALSE COUNTERATTACK – PARRY-RIPOSTE – While retreating from an opponent who is on the *march*, the fencer can make a false counterattack to provoke the attacker to finish his attack (perhaps with a lunge). The fencer who made the false counterattack can then make a *parry-riposte*. He can also *pull distance* and start his own attack. This is often done as a method of finishing a *push-pull* situation. The advantage to this strategy is that the defending fencer has some influence on when and where on the strip the attacker finishes with his lunge. He is saying, essentially, "Attack me when I'm ready instead of when you are." *Defensive second intention* can also be used this way. The difference between the two is that the false counterattack will usually provoke a direct attack while the defensive second intention (false parry and real parry) will usually provoke an indirect attack.

GET-AWAY-GO, PULLING DISTANCE, TAKING OVER THE ATTACK – The defending fencer retreats to avoid being hit by an attack and then immediately launches his own attack. This requires a good sense of distance, the ability to accelerate footwork, and a good sense of timing. This strategy can substitute for the parry riposte on the tactical wheel, but is vulnerable to a long attack. (You may occasionally hear this incorrectly called a "distance parry and riposte.")

PUSH-PULL – This is a footwork strategy. The fencer first pushes his opponent back by taking the initiative and advancing. If he is unable to successfully attack, or is unwilling to risk making an attack (against the opponent who may have a very strong defense), he can then give up right of way by breaking off his attack and begin retreating. This pulls the opponent forward, who will most likely try to establish right of way. The fencer using the push-pull, who is now retreating, can make an *attack in preparation* if the opponent has not established *right of way*. If he does establish right of way, then he can make a *parry-riposte*, or *false counterattack – parry-riposte*, or *defensive second intention*, or even a *counterattack* if the situation allows.

*ATTACK IN PREPARATION – An attack made during the opponent's *preparation*. The skill to time and execute successful attacks into preparation (sense of *tempo*) is said to be one of the marks of a truly skilled foilist. For example: the opponent advances and the fencer retreats. The opponent attempts a simple direct attack with advance lunge, but momentarily pulls back the arm during the advance. At that moment, the fencer attacks with a lunge. The opponent finishes his advance-lunge, and both fencers are hit. Our fencer has made a successful attack in preparation and scores a point. If our fencer had waited a fraction of a second longer to attack, the opponent's arm would have started forward again and the opponent would have had **ROW** and scored the touch.

It is also an attack in preparation if the fencer attacks while the opponent is *on the march* and his arm is not extending or his point is not threatening the fencer's valid target.

17.6. More Fencing Terms

This section includes definitions and discussions of terms used elsewhere but not previously defined as well as definitions and discussions of useful terms not previously mentioned.

*Angulation – Directing the foil at an angle to the target instead of straight forward. Angulation bypasses parries or ensures that the tip digs into target that does not face the fencer, such as the sides or back.

Appel – A sharp, quick stamp of the front foot on the floor. *See p. 60.*

Arrest – A *stop thrust. See p. 92.*

Armorer - An armorer is a person skilled in fixing fencing equipment. Is your electric foil not working? An armorer can fix it. Is your electric foil in 2 or 3 pieces? With the right parts, an armorer can fix it. Armorers also inspect equipment to prevent cheating in competitions. Obviously fencers are all honorable and well-meaning individuals and none of them cheat! From time to time, however, equipment doesn't conform to the rules, and the armorers keep an eye out for that during their inspections. Finally, and most importantly, armorers are important for ensuring that the fencers stay safe while fencing. For instance, they examine and test fencing masks at competitions to be sure that they are strong and in good repair so that the mask can do its job properly. If an armorer tests your mask and it fails, he will tell you that you cannot use that mask ever again. You'll need another mask. Rather than getting upset at him because you'll have to buy a new mask, you should thank him for his help and recognize that he just might have saved your life. Whether or not you become an armorer, you should learn how to take care of your own equipment. If you are lucky enough to have an armorer, coach, or fencer at your club who can rewire weapons and fix equipment like body cords then be sure to learn as much as you can about armoring from him. There are also books, DVD's, and clinics taught around the country where you can learn repair skills. For those who wish to learn a great deal about armoring and also receive certification in it, the USFA has offered courses in armoring, called Armorers College. Treat a good armorer as you would your best friend – he's worth his weight in gold.

*Black Card – A *penalty* given by the referee that removes the recipient from the competition. This is the most severe penalty, given for offenses like cheating and brutality. *See Penalty.*

*Cards – Cards are shown by the *referee* to indicate warnings or penalties. *See penalty.*

CLASSICAL FENCING – A cousin of modern sport fencing. Classical fencers use non-electric foils, epees, and sabers and follow rules that resemble those used in fencing before the electrical scoring system gained in popularity. Some classical fencers employ the techniques of the middle-to-late 19th Century; others include those of the early 20th. Classical fencing emphasizes form and technique over athleticism and tactics, and is generally fenced in a more defensive manner than modern sport fencing. The key question for classical fencers is "What if it were sharp?"

Well-trained classical and sport fencers speak the same language (attack and defense with foils, sabers, or epees) but with different accents and rules of grammar.

CLOSING A LINE – Moving one's blade into a *parry position* so as to prevent an attack to the target protected by that parry. *Compare Opening a Line, Line.*

CLOSING THE DISTANCE – Decreasing the distance from one's opponent. *Compare Opening the Distance, Keeping the Distance, Pulling Distance, Collapsing the Distance.*

*CORPS-Á-CORPS – Body contact between fencers. It is cause for a "Halt!" in all three weapons and the fencer who causes it is penalized with a *yellow card* in foil and saber.

COUNTERATTACK WITH EVASION – See "Evasion with Counterattack."

*CUE – In a drill or a lesson, an action or situation that provokes the student to respond.

DEFENSE BY DISTANCE – Thwarting an attack by retreating so as to make it fall short. *Compare Pulling Distance, Getaway-Go.*

DEROBEMENT – An offensive or counteroffensive action which consists of deceiving an *attack on the blade* or a *prise de fer (take)*, generally by means of a *disengage*. It is frequently understood as being immediately followed by a *thrust.*

DIRECT – An offensive or counteroffensive action in which the blade begins, stays, and ends in the same line.

DIRECTOR – An older word for the referee. That's why we named Michael Curtiz as the referee of our imaginary pool on pages 52 – 53: he directed swashbuckler movies like *Captain Blood, The Sea Hawk,* and *The Adventures of Robin Hood.* Curtiz, by the way, claimed (implausibly) to have fenced for Hungary in the 1912 Olympics.

EN GARDE – French for "on guard," and pronounced nearly the same.

*DRY – Fencing without the use of an electrical scoring machine. In Britain, called **"STEAM."**

*ELECTRIC – Ekectruc fencing: fencing with the help of the electrical scoring system; electric foil, saber, epee, etc.: equipment designed for use with the electrical scoring system. *Compare Dry.*

*Epee – A fencing weapon with a three-sided blade that uses the point to score touches. The target area is the entire body of the opponent. Epee fencing does not use rules of right of way.

Evasions, Evasions with Counterattack - These are any ducks, twists, displacements, and dodges (other than movement backward) that move the body away from the threatening blade. A few specific actions have been named.

Demi-volte – an evasion consisting of a defensive half turn of the body used to avoid being hit.

Inquartata – an evasion with counterattack used against an attack to the inside line. It consists of a half turn made by moving the rear foot to the right (for a right-handed fencer), while *counterattacking with opposition* in the line of four.

Passata sotto – an evasion with counterattack to low line with a reverse lunge while ducking with the upper body and placing the fingers of the non-weapon hand on the floor for support.

Intagliata – the inverse of the inquartata, it is done against an attack to the outside high line and consists of a half-turn made by moving the rear foot to the left, accompanied by a counterattack in 3 or 6 opposition.

Although these actions are occasionally overlooked by modern fencers as being obsolete, the named evasions are still used with some success today, and they all have modern variants. They are worth trying.

*Fencing – The art, practice or sport using a sword for both defense and offense.

Fencing Line – The line connecting the front heels of the two fencers.

Fencing Time – *See Tempo, Time.*

*FIE – Fédération Internationale d'Escrime (International Fencing Federation). The FIE is the international governing body of fencing. It makes all the rules and oversees international competitions. FIE-approved equipment is required for international competitions.

*First Position, Ready Position – This is the traditional body position during the salute. The fencer stands erect with feet at ninety degrees and heels touching. The torso is turned with the weapon shoulder somewhat forward and both arms are down.

Flat – In foil and epee, an attack (or riposte, or counterattack) that lands with the side of the blade or barrel instead of the tip, and therefore does not trigger the scoring machine or score a point. In the days before the electrical apparatus, it was necessary to distinguish between two kinds of flat hits:

PASSÉ – A thrust that slides along the surface of the target rather than hitting with the point.

PLAQUÉ – A thrust that hits with the side of the blade and tip, rather than with the point.

*FOIL – A fencing weapon with a four-sided blade that uses the point to score touches. The target area is the torso of the opponent. Foil fencing uses rules of *right of way*. See Fig. 2, "Practice Foils."

FLECHE – *See p. 64*

FLICK – A thrust delivered by whipping the arm, wrist, and blade to make the foible and tip arc toward the target and score. The tip can land perpendicular to the target (i.e., straight on) even when the middle of the blade and forte are parallel to the target. The flick allows the fencer to hit target area that is inaccessible to a straight thrust, such as the sides or back of the shoulder. Traditional parry positions have little success in blocking flick attacks, and *shielding parries* were developed to counter them. Flicking was very popular, if not overused, from the 1980's to 2005. In that year, a change in the timing of the scoring machine made flicks far more difficult, though still possible.

GENUINE ACTION – An action that is intended to score.

HISTORICAL FENCING – Historical fencing is different from modern *sport fencing* and to some extent from *classical fencing*. Historical fencers study and replicate sword fighting from various historical time periods such as the Middle Ages and Renaissance and may use period-accurate replica swords such as rapiers, two-handed broadswords, and even non-sword weapons like daggers, pole arms, and spears. This often requires the use of armor. Many historical fencers are scholarly historians while others simply enjoy beating on their friends with big swords.

*INDIRECT – An offensive or counteroffensive action ending in a different line than the line of initiation. For example, a disengage attack may start with the blade in the high inside line but score in the high outside line.

KEEPING THE DISTANCE – Maintaining the distance from one's opponent. *Compare Closing the Distance, Opening the Distance.*

*LINES – "Line" and "Lines" have several meanings:

(1) **LINES OF TARGET**: areas of one's own and the opponent's target defined by their relation to the hand. Relative location of the fencers' blades and target area creates up to four areas of target, using combinations of high/low and inside/outside.

(2) **LINES OF ATTACK**: positions of the blade and point which threaten a line of the target. *Compare Fencing Line, Point in Line, Change of Line.*

MAINTAINING THE DISTANCE – *Keeping the distance.*

MANEUVERING – Moving backward and forward and from side to side on the strip with *preparations*, changing distance and direction, to gain advantage. *Compare Preparation.*

MARAGING STEEL – A high-strength, low-carbon steel with a specialized crystalline structure, produced by annealing and precipitation hardening (called "aging." The name comes from that of the developer of the crystalline structure, Adolf *Martens*, plus *aging*. Most, but not all *FIE-certified* blades are made of Maraging steel.

OLYMPIC FENCING – Fencing under *FIE* rules as practiced in the Olympic Games. *See Sport Fencing, and compare Classical Fencing, Historical Fencing, Stage Fencing.*

OPENING A LINE – Moving one's blade out of a *parry position* so as to make an attack in that *line* possible. *Compare Line, Closing a Line.*

OPENING THE DISTANCE – Increasing the distance from one's opponent. *Compare closing the distance, maintaining the distance.*

OUT OF LINE – Said of a blade that is not threatening valid target, or that has been moved from its original position by the opponent's blade.

PREPARATION – A fencing action that prepares for an action that will be used to score. This includes footwork and bladework. From the point of view of *Right of Way*, it is important to distinguish preparations from real *attacks*.

*PENALTY – Improper fencing or improper behavior brings penalties. The penalties include loss of ground on the strip, a warning *(yellow card)* the cancellation (annulment) of a touch scored, the award of a touch for the opponent *(red card)*, and exclusion from the competition and/or from the *venue* (the scene of the competition) *(black card)*. Fencers who have received a *yellow card* or a *red card* for an offense will receive a *red card* for any other yellow-card offense in that bout. *Red Cards* are also given for a group of more serious offenses. *Black cards* entail expulsion from the competition, and/or the venue, and/or the tournament. They are given for serious offenses against sportsmanship, safety, and order. Warnings and black cards may be issued against spectators.

Fencers are urged to study at least the penalty chart in the rulebook before entering their first competition. The explanation given here is necessarily condensed and incomplete. Ignorance of the rules is no excuse.

*Piste — the fencing *strip.*

*Ready position - *See First position.*

*Red Card — A *penalty* given by the referee equivalent to a point for the opponent. Red cards are given for the second occurrence of a *yellow card* offense and immediately for more serious violations.

Remise, Reprise, *Redoublement — There is widespread disagreement about the application of these terms. The FIE Rulebook defines them as follows:

> a) The remise: A simple and immediate offensive action which follows the original attack, without withdrawing the arm, after the opponent has parried or retreated, when the latter has either quitted contact with the blade without riposting or has made a riposte which is delayed, indirect or compound.
>
> b) The redoublement: A new action, either simple or compound, made against an opponent who has parried without riposting or who has merely avoided the first action by retreating or displacing the target.
>
> c) The reprise of the attack: A new attack executed immediately after a return to the on guard position.

The French Fencing Federation, however, specifies that the remise must be in the same line as the original attack, defines the reprise as a second offensive action made immediately after an attack, without referring to a return to the on guard position, and *defines the redoublement the way the FIE rulebook defines the reprise,* adding that the new offensive action after the return to the on guard position is made with a lunge or fleche.

William Gaugler's very useful *Fencing Terminology* cites an array of French treatises that exhibit even greater variation.

The situation is complicated by the Italian term *raddoppio,* which translates as "redoublement." In the Italian school the redoublement refers to the action of the legs, which come close together before any attack or retaking of attack in order to cover a greater distance than that of a simple advance. The Italians call the lunge – recover forward – lunge a reprise of lunge *(ripresa d'affondo.)*

For the definitions used in this book, see p. 88-89. Which terminology is correct? *The one your coach uses!*

*Referee — The official who oversees a fencing bout. Formerly called a *director.*

*Right of Way (ROW) – A set of rules in foil and saber which prevent both fencers from scoring at the same time. If both fencers are touched at about the same time, the *ROW* rules determine who gets the touch.

*Saber – A fencing weapon that uses the point and edge of the blade to score touches. The target area is the torso, mask, and arms (but not hands) of the opponent. Saber fencing uses rules of right of way.

Salle – The fencing room or the fencing club. Short for the French *"Salle d'armes,"* the fencing hall.

*Salute – The courteous and respectful motion of the sword done at the beginning and end of each fencing match or lesson. Fencers salute each other as well as the referee and spectators. The traditional salute is done in first position and begins with presenting the blade forward to the recipient of the salute and then drawing it back to the face, and then slashing downward and forward. Some fencers put their own individual embellishment into their salutes, but excessive displays such as bowing or slashing a "Z" in the air like Zorro are generally frowned upon.

Shielding Parry – A parry that blocks a *coupé* or *flick* in foil or a cutting action in saber by physically blocking the opponent's blade, which is moving at an angle instead of a straight thrusting motion.

*Simple – An *action* using one motion in one *tempo*.

Sport Fencing, Olympic Fencing – The modern sport of fencing as discussed in this book. Sport fencing emphasizes athleticism, winning within the rules and conventions, and the gaining of local, national, and international championships. Internationally, it is governed by the *FIE;* nationally, by the *USFA*.

Stage Fencing, Theatrical Fencing, Stage Combat, Movie Fencing, Fight Choreography – The goal in this type of fencing is to entertain and amaze the audience with realistic looking but perfectly safe swordplay. The actors train many hours memorizing the fight sequences with blunt swords. They generally focus on hitting each other's sword instead of each other's body.

Fencing as a sport may not be as popular as baseball or football in the U.S. but fencing is everywhere in our theater, movies, and television. Stage fights are choreographed. Without stage fight choreographers we wouldn't have swordfights in our movies like *The Princess Bride* and *Star Wars* or in plays like *Romeo and Juliet.*

Steam – See *Dry.*

*Strip – Also called the *piste,* the strip is the area in which a *bout* takes place. A full-size strip is 14 meters (about 46 feet) long and 1.5 to 2.0 meters (about 5 to 6.5 feet) wide. It is marked by a center line, two on guard lines, each 2 meters from the center, and two warning lines, each 2 meters from the end of the strip. Before each touch, the fencers place themselves **on guard** on the on guard lines. If a fencer goes off the side of the strip with one or both feet, a halt is called and the opponent gains a meter. If a fencer goes off the back of the strip with both feet, or is forced to go on guard with both feet off the strip, his opponent gains a touch. See the diagram on *p. 36*.

TEMPO, TIME – A set of terms with multiple and overlapping meanings:

*TEMPO

(1) The time it takes to do one action or make one fencing motion. This is independent of the amount of actual clock time that the action takes to complete. A slow extension of the arm takes one tempo. A fast extension of the arm takes one tempo.

(2) *Time* (see below).

(3) *Sense of tempo = Sense of time.*

*TIME

(1) The amount of clock time within which a fencing bout must be finished: three minutes plus one possible minute of overtime for a 5-touch bout, three 3-minute periods separated by a minute's rest, plus one possible minute of overtime for a 15-touch bout, nine 3-minute periods for a team match.

(2) The right moment to begin a fencing action. An action "in time" has *Right of Way*. A fencer with a "sense of time" has a feeling for when to begin an action.

(3) Used concerning counteroffensive actions: a "time thrust" is a *counterattack* with *opposition*; a *countertime* action is an action against a counterattack. Go figure.

(4) **IN TIME, OUT OF TIME** – Said of offensive actions, especially counterattacks, that have – or lack – *ROW*. "The attack is from the right; the counterattack was out of time," or "*Preparation* from the right; *counterattack* in time from the left."

(5) **BROKEN TIME** - Said of an offensive action made with a deliberate pause in order to confuse the opponent's sense of rhythm and/or to draw a premature parry.

*TRANSPORT, TRANSFER – See *Prise de Fer*. The transport is an action on the opponent's blade that carries (transports) the opponent's blade from one line to another without losing contact. Transports can be *diagonal, semicircular, or circular – bind, croisé, or envelopment.*

USFA, (THE UNITED STATES FENCING ASSOCIATION, USA FENCING) – The national governing body (NGB) of sport fencing in the U.S. The USFA sets the rules of the sport (usually following the rules set by the FIE), holds competitions for fencers across the country, and publishes the quarterly magazine *American Fencing*.

VALID TARGET AREA, TARGET AREA – The parts of the fencer's target area on which a touch can be scored. *For foil, see the illustration on page 36. For saber and epee, see the discussions of those weapons.*

YELLOW CARD – A *penalty* given by the referee equivalent to a verbal warning. This is the least severe penalty. The second yellow card offense draws a *Red Card. See Penalties.*

18. Quizzes

Answers may be found by reviewing the materials in this book.

Exam I

Each question is worth 10 points. A score of 80% is required for passing.

Answer any five:

1) A practice foil is built from what parts?

2) The blade is divided into sections. Name them and tell how they differ in function or use.

3) What is Right of Way? What is the purpose of Right of Way?

4) Which parries close the low inside line?

5) What is the purpose of the feint attack? Why would you use it?

6) What is the job of the referee?

Demonstrate and describe five of the following:

1) On guard, advance, retreat, and lunge.

2) The three simple attacks.

3) The bind or diagonal transfer.

4) Beat-feint – deceive (beat followed by a feint attack)

5) Parry-ripostes, both direct and indirect.

6) A situation in which the counterattack would score a point.

Exam 2

Each question is worth 10 points. A score of 80% is required for passing.

Answer any five:

1) What is the tactical wheel? What good is it?

2) What is a preparation?

3) What is first intention? What is second intention?

4) Tell three ways you could get your opponent to attack you.

5) What are the advantages and disadvantages of a feint attack?

6) Why would you use second intention? Why wouldn't you use it?

Demonstrate and describe 5 of the following:

1) Parries 1, 2, 4, 6, 7 and 8.

2) Multiple feint attack.

3) The difference between an indirect attack and a feint attack.

4) First intention, second intention, and feint attacks all with the same initial action.

5) Two ways to provoke or influence your opponent with bladework.

6) How does Right of Way change from person to person?

19. Websites for Fencers

ASKFRED: WWW.ASKFRED.NET

AskFred is the *Fencing REsults Database*. It us used by competition and camp hosts to advertise their events and to allow interested fencers to register for them online. Fencers likewise use AskFred to find competitions to attend. When the competitions have been completed the event hosts usually post the results here as well. The results are not official, however, until submitted to the USFA.

FEDERATION INTERNATIONALE D' ESCRIME: WWW.FIE.CH

The FIE is the international governing body of fencing. They make all the rules. The FIE website has information about international competitions, inspirational pictures and videos, as well as the rules, documents, and information about their meetings. You can truly get the sense that fencing is an international sport from visiting this website. Beginner fencers should be aware of its existence and is worth visiting for the videos.

FENCING.NET: WWW.FENCING.NET

Fencing.net is an excellent resource for all things fencing including up-to-date news. It also has several fencing discussion forums where fencers share advice and information about competitions, strategies, coaching, equipment repair, fencing politics, etc. On the forums, it is best to first use the search function to see if the topic you are interested in has already been discussed. Fencing.net also sells equipment.

THE UNITED STATES FENCING ASSOCIATION: HTTP://USFENCING.ORG

The USFA is the national governing body of fencing in the United States. It oversees and organizes competitions, develops and selects teams for international competition, and has offered coaching training through its Coaches College. All fencers should be members of the USFA so that they can receive *American Fencing* magazine, benefit from accident insurance coverage, and compete at USFA competitions. The USFA website has all the forms and documents you could want, such as the rulebook, score sheets, parents' handbook, and ratings chart, plus pictures and videos, and a listing of member clubs around the country. The USFA also goes by the name of USA Fencing.

THE UNITED STATES FENCING COACHES ASSOCIATION: WWW.USFCA.ORG

This is the national professional governing body for fencing coaches in the United States. It offers coaching training clinics around the country and examines and certifies coaches. It is affiliated with the International Academy of Arms and is the only organization in the U.S. that can certify coaches as Fencing Masters.

THE UNITED STATES FENCING HALL OF FAME: HTTP://USFENCINGHALLOFFAME.COM

THE MUSEUM OF AMERICAN FENCING: MUSEUMOFAMERICANFENCING.COM

Men and women who have reached the highest level of achievement and have made important contributions to the sport of fencing are honored in the US Fencing Hall of Fame. The Museum of American Fencing is a fascinating collection of important records, photos, articles, and trivia relating to the past and present of our sport.

WHEELCHAIR FENCER: WWW.WHEELCHAIRFENCER.ORG

Yes, fencing is done in wheelchairs, and it is both inspiring and amazing. The chairs are locked down into a frame. Wheelchair fencing is part of the Paralympic Games. Able-bodied fencers who are recovering from leg or foot injuries are often advised to train sitting down and will benefit from an understanding of wheelchair fencing.

YOUTUBE: WWW.YOUTUBE.COM

YouTube is a popular video hosting website where you can find videos from fencing competitions and even fencing lessons, as well as just about everything non-fencing too. YouTube hosts an increasing number of fencing channels. But be careful: quality varies.

20. Fencing Equipment Vendors

As a fencer, coach, and club owner I have purchased lots of equipment over the years from many different suppliers. Even though my club usually purchases from one particular vendor, I still have to shop around for certain hard to find or specialty items. It is good to be aware of what the different companies offer. Most will have their own brand name as well as equipment from other manufacturers. A pair of Brand X fencing shoes, for instance, will be the same from any of the vendors, so it pays to shop around for the best price. Price is not the only factor, though, and you may find that one or a few vendors earn your loyalty as a customer with their service. I strongly recommend learning how to assemble and repair your own fencing weapons and keeping a toolbox well stocked with parts and tools.

The following list is incomplete. You can use Google or USFencing.org to find more vendors.

Absolute Fencing Gear: www.absolutefencinggear.com
Alliance Fencing Equipment: www.alliancefencingequipment.com
American Fencers Supply: www.amfence.com
Balestra Fencing: www.balestrafencing.com/
Blade Fencing Equipment: www.blade-fencing.com
Blue Gauntlet: www.blue-gauntlet.com
Escrime USA: www.escrimeusa.com
FenceSmart: www.fencesmart.net/
Fencing.net: www.fencing.net
Fencing Footage: www.fencingfootage.com
The Fencing Post: www.thefencing.post.com
Leon Paul: www.leonpaulusa.com
Physical Chess: www.physicalchess.com
SKA Swordplay Books: www.swordplaybooks.com
Sword Masters: www.sword-masters.com
Triplette Competition Arms: www.triplette.com
Victory Fencing Gear: www.victoryfencinggear.com
Zivkovic Modern Fencing Equipment: www.zivkovic.com

(And check out *amazon.com* and *eBay.com* for their numerous fencing offers.)

Conclusion: A Personal Thought

As we grow up our parents tell us to be good little boys and girls. They tell us to be kind and gentle. They tell us to help others instead of hurt them. They tell us to play fair and be honest. Then we become fencers. We are supposed to be honorable, courteous and gracious off the strip, but finally we lower our masks and our faces are hidden. We become something different, something most people will never get to experience. We awaken and become artful, aggressive, focused, powerful, cunning, beautiful, deceptive, awe-inspiring, poetic, manipulative, graceful, and deadly. We lie to our opponents with our feints, symbolically injure them with our blunted but very real steel swords, and we then rob them of their spirit with our victories over them. We also suffer our own defeats, which are necessary for us if we are to value our hard earned victories. We take risks and find excitement from not knowing whether we'll be rewarded or punished by taking them. Occasionally, no, rarely, we find ourselves so in tune with our bodies and our opponent's actions that time crystallizes into a moment of perfection and we feel as if we have overcome our human limitations – and then we lift our masks and it is all gone, like a dream that leaves us covered in sweat and our hands shaking. Without our masks hiding who we really are, we go back to being the good citizens our parents told us to be. Fencing isn't just a fun game to play; it tests us and allows us to tap into our combative and competitive human nature, to do and be those things our parents rightly tell us to avoid … and get rewarded and praised for it.

CPSIA information can be obtained at www.ICGtesting.com
Printed in the USA
LVOW021428150213

320336LV00001B/32/P

9 780978 902254